WENNER–GREN CENTER
INTERNATIONAL SYMPOSIUM SERIES

VOLUME 13

THE POSSIBILITIES
OF CHARTING MODERN LIFE

THE POSSIBILITIES OF CHARTING MODERN LIFE

*A Symposium for Ethnological
Research about Modern Time in Stockholm
March 1967*

EDITED BY

SIGURD ERIXON †

assisted by

GRETA ARWIDSSON and HARALD HVARFNER

PERGAMON PRESS

OXFORD · LONDON · EDINBURGH · NEW YORK
TORONTO · SYDNEY · PARIS · BRAUNSCHWEIG

Pergamon Press Ltd., Headington Hill Hall, Oxford
4 & 5 Fitzroy Square, London W.1
Pergamon Press (Scotland) Ltd., 2 & 3 Teviot Place, Edinburgh 1
Pergamon Press Inc., Maxwell House, Fairview Park, Elmsford, New York 10523
Pergamon of Canada Ltd., 207 Queen's Quay West, Toronto 1
Pergamon Press (Aust.) Pty. Ltd., 19A Boundary Street,
Rushcutters Bay, N.S.W. 2011, Australia
Pergamon Press S.A.R.L., 24 rue des Écoles, Paris 5e
Vieweg & Sohn GmbH, Burgplatz 1, Braunschweig

First Edition 1970
Library of Congress Catalog Card No. 78-78907

Printed in Hungary

08 013308 8

CONTENTS

Translation pp 1—146 Donald Burton
      pp 147—172 Matt T. Salo

SIGURD ERIXON
1888—1968

SIGURD ERIXON: IN MEMORIAM

JOHN GRANLUND

Institute of Folklife Research, the
Nordiska Museet and the University of Stockholm

SIGURD ERIXON, professor of Scandinavian and comparative folklife research at the Nordiska Museet and Stockholm University, died on the 18th February 1968. He was born at Söderköping in Östergötland on the 26th March, 1888. In 1914 he was appointed an assistant at the Nordiska Museet, in 1922 assistant keeper of the peasant department of the same museum, in 1924 head of the department of culture history at the open-air museum of Skansen, and in 1929 head of the department of peasant culture of the Nordiska Museet. He was also university teacher and examiner in his subject from 1927, in which year he passed his filosofie licentiat-examination at Uppsala University. In 1934 he was appointed professor of Nordic ethnology (from 1945 called Nordic and comparative folklife research) at the Nordiska Museet and Stockholm University. Also after his retirement in 1955 he was very actively engaged in research work and the organizing of new research enterprises.

With the death of Sigurd Erixon ended the career of a scholar and teacher of unusual proportions. From his youth he belonged to the type of students who made themselves thoroughly acquainted with the Scandinavian languages, not through armchair studies, but as recorders in the field, of Swedish dialects, often with their native regions as points of departure. This linguistic training in connection with studies of archaeology and with archaeologic field work as well as complementary studies in the history of Swedish art under the guidance of its nestor Johnny Roosval, provided the fundamental basis for Sigurd Erixon's own independent and multifaceted field researches in the new area, Scandinavian ethnology.

From the beginning two lines may be discerned in Sigurd Erixon's scientific work. On one side his studies follow a formal typologic trend and resulted in investigations of Swedish types of villages, farm layouts, houses, furniture and home equipment, house building details, such as corner joint techniques in log building and door-jambs, tools and implements of different kinds etc. He always tries to locate every different type in time and space and also, whenever this was possible, in its social

milieu. On the other side he may also be called an adept of culture anthropology, that line which departs from the Germano-American ethnographer
Franz Boas and his great contemporaries and which aimed at penetrating
the whole culture complex of society. Sigurd Erixon applied such views,
though naturally with national limitations, already in 1912 in his first
field work in the parish of Kila in Östergötland, published after complementary investigations in 1946 under the title of "Kila, en östgötsk skogsby". Its most monumental expression this line found in "Skultuna bruks
historia" (History of the brass works of Skultuna), the first part of which
was printed in 1921, the second in 1935, the third (written by Erik Falk)
in 1953, and the fourth (written by Sven Ljung in cooperation with
Sigurd Erixon) in 1957. A fifth volume was to deal with the living conditions and wages of the brass workers of Skultuna and was in course of
preparation, when the pen fell from the hand of this indefatigable researcher. "Skultuna bruks historia" can never be taken as a model by
those who intend to write a doctor's thesis, but unintentionally, owing
to its author's original working methods, it nevertheless provides an
almost encyclopaedic knowledge of the urban and rural complex represented by this Central Swedish industry, that is to say, the mutual relations between the cultures of an industrial and rural region under the
influence of directive rules from the central administration.

If we keep to these two main lines, the life of Sigurd Erixon as a researcher becomes a unit. It cannot be described in all details here. We see
him first as the energetic museum official, collecting objects and documents apt to illustrate the past. When in 1943 the Swedish Society of
Anthropology and Geography conferred upon him the distinguished
J. K. Wahlberg medal in gold, special reference was made to his intensive
contributions in connection with the preparations for the Jubilee exhibition of Gothenburg in 1923. This work had been started by Sigurd
Erixon already in 1918 for the sections of handicrafts, industry and rural
life at the Exhibition. As collaborators he took a number of young
students; many of them later on became academic teachers and heads
of institutions. With great eagerness they crisscrossed the West Swedish
provinces and enriched the Museum of Gothenburg with invaluable
collections of material objects and records. Such collecting and recording
work was at that time the first and last duty of every museum
man.

It has often been remarked that around 1900 the study of national
history had become almost a duty, which in a way may be related to the
regionalism that was a constituent element of the Romantic currents

of that time. By that time, however, the romantic view on history was already gliding over into a sturdy realism.

Like his friend Sigurd Wallin, head of the department for urban and upper social classes at the Nordiska Museet, and the great contemporaries Sigurd Curman, State antiquary of Sweden 1923–1946, and Johnny Roosval, prominent representative of modern art research in Sweden, who put on record town buildings, churches, vicarages and manor houses, Sigurd Erixon intended his inventories of rural building culture in villages and farms to be a contribution to the preservation of cultural monuments and traditions. Nowadays the initiative in this respect does not lie with the Nordiska Museet, as was often the case in earlier times. With its vast collections this museum now is rather a storehouse of information in the service of public activities in this field, which were and in many ways still are supported by interested private institutions and persons.

Sigurd Erixon's appointment as an academic teacher already in 1927 involved a new initiative. The docentship in folklife research at Uppsala university was out of function owing to the illness of its holder. The chair of Nordic and comparative folklife research at the Nordiska Museet, constituted in 1918, was purely a research institution and its holder did not teach. For a long time special permission was necessary for passing an examination in this subject of study. It was Sigurd Erixon who created the intimate and effective contacts between the Nordiska Museet and the present Stockholm University, which in 1934 led to an agreement according to which the professorship was combined with regular teaching and examination at the university. The position was further strengthened by the creation in 1941 of the still existing Institute for folklife research in Stockholm.

Sigurd Erixon was not only a renewer in his field of study. He was also a successful editor of many scientific publications, such as *Folk-Liv* which with its 30 volumes has made Swedish ethnology respected in Europe and also in the United States, *Nordisk Kultur* with 30 volumes, *Svenska Kulturbilder* with 12 volumes, *Liv och Folkkultur* with 8 volumes, the journal *Laos* with 3 volumes and many more. It was Sigurd Erixon's unique capacity as an organizer which above all made all this learned activity possible. Long before he had founded the Institute for folklife research, which made Villa Lusthusporten a stronghold for researchers from far and near, he had in 1916 started the Village Research section of the Nordiska Museet. It was during the latter half of the 1920's transformed into the Ethnologic Research department of the museum which from 1926 obtained financial support from a special public fund and from July 1st 1938 more permanent state allowances.

Sigurd Erixon was a highly dynamic personality, his character was that of an individualist, a leader and "entrepreneur". His production of weighty scientific works is most comprehensive. In scientific reviews, such as *Fataburen, Rig, Ymer,* etc., he has published a great many papers, always characterized by new viewpoints and rich source material. In his large general surveys we may find many statements and conceptions which not always are the results of a cogent logic but very often the fruit of intuition. He once said to me when I was a young amanuensis: "To draw the correct conclusions from a small material, that is where the skill comes in." In his great aperçus he has often given proofs of this skill. In the carto-graphic work "Atlas över Svensk Folkkultur" the overwhelming quantity of registered data sometimes seems to have been brought together at the expense of its quality.

After the end of World War II Sigurd Erixon intensified his international activities, which had long before been a main interest with him. They were in a way focused on the Commission internationale des arts et traditions populaires (CIAP) which had been founded in Prague in 1928, under the sponsorship of the Institut international de coopération intel-lectuelle of the League of Nations. To the projects which were realized through the CIAP belong two important volumes of the *International Dictionary of Regional European Ethnology and Folklore,* as well as the journal *Laos.* A point of culmination with regard to the position of Swedish ethnology in Europe was the International Congress of European and Western Ethnology in Stockholm in August 1951, which was held in the name of the CIAP. CIAP was formally dissolved at Athens in 1964 but Erixon's international activities were continued through the so-called "Hässelby group" consisting of leading ethnologists from Western and Eastern Europe and with participants also from the United States. Its aims were threefold: to prepare a handbook of European ethnology, to arrange yearly conferences, and to publish the review *Ethnologia Europaea,* three issues of which have appeared up till now. Three conferences have been arranged hitherto: the first at Hässelby near Stockholm in 1965, the second at Julita in 1966, and the third at Utstein kloster in Norway in 1967. For the symposium of Lissabon in July 1968 a publication in honour of Sigurd Erixon and printed as an issue of *Ethnologia Europaea* was being prepared. It will now be published in his memory.

Sigurd Erixon and many of his generation grew up within and created around them a kind of pioneering spirit, we might call it the "Gründer-zeit" of ethnology. They have left us in charge of a great and responsible heritage to administer and pass on to those who will follow.

INTRODUCTION

AT ITS regular session on 12 March 1966 "The Nordic Council for Anthropological Research", Stockholm, decided to arrange a symposium for modern anthropological research. This was held at the Wenner-Gren Centre in Stockholm on 7–11 March 1967. The Committee appointed to realize the symposium considered that general ethnology should be given the same possibilities as European regional ethnology, with regard both to theoretical questions and to the exemplification of the material. It was not considered appropriate to make too strict a division between theoretical questions and concrete investigations.

The task for this working symposium was to discuss the possibilities of applying the same methods for the study of the present as have hitherto been applied in the ethnology concentrated upon history, and to consider whether new approaches to the problems and new methods were needed which might perhaps be contrary to the historical ones.

For the European folklife scientist the situation has been rather radically changed in many respects, for example through the greater dependence of modern culture on central control and influences from outside, the rapidity with which innovations are accepted, the adjustment or elimination of local boundaries, and, finally, profound modifications in the psychological field, in the social structure formerly existing and in culture itself. In some ways the situation is the same for general ethnology (anthropology), even if the non-European peoples are contributing more self-evident information on account of their dependence on local conditions and natural assets.

One desideratum is that modern ethnological methods should be more closely defined, and that the treatment of local working fields should be discussed, for example through the recording of changes in a particular field in stages by marking off suitable dates. To this must be added the increased need for research by individuals, with grouping and comparisons. In this connection the modern neighbour sciences ought to be considered and a delimitation towards them indicated.

The problems involved are to a great extent international, and with regard to the North the European perspectives will be decisive.

SIGURD ERIXON

ADDRESS OF WELCOME

I BEG herewith to bid the Symposium of The Nordic Council for Anthropological Research, on the subject "Anthropological Research on the Present", a hearty welcome. We shall for some days devote ourselves to lectures and discussions on a subject of lively concern to us all, that is, the relation of our sciences to the modern era and even to the actual present. From the lectures sent in it is already apparent that we are not altogether in agreement but are in part of divided opinion. It is to be hoped, however, that we are not so egocentric or fanatical that we have not a good deal to learn from one another.

The questions we shall be discussing are as a matter of fact extremely important and may to a certain extent assume decisive importance. Let us then set to work with purposeful will and earnestness, but also in the spirit of goodwill and respect for each others' opinions and results that has hitherto generally prevailed among us, at least where it has been a matter of responsible contributions. We have a fine Nordic tradition to maintain in this connection. May this tradition keep us in good humour even if ideas clash and some shots are fired. In my opinion it should be possible for this symposium to become a sort of roll-call and inspection of the researchers. Irrespective of whether our heart inclines to the one or other quarter, we should ventilate a series of problems with tolerance and understanding.

That it is I who bid you welcome may perhaps be regarded as an indication that our researchers do not only demand to hear the views of the young and the youngest.

SIGURD ERIXON

ETHNOLOGICAL INVESTIGATION
OF THE PRESENT

SIGURD ERIXON †

THE investigation of the age in which we live constitutes a natural part of folklife research and has been carried on as long as such research has existed. As a rule, however, it is the retrospective slant that has been predominant. What has been taken as the point of departure has been a present-day stage whose duration has been dependent on actions and decisions of a particular kind, and this stage has then been compared with older conditions. In our country it is the legislated agrarian reform of 1827, the enactment concerning compulsory elementary school as from 1842, the extension of the freedom of trade and production in various respects as from 1846, the advent of the railways in 1856, the victorious advance of industrialism as from the 1870's, the general adoption of monetary economy and so forth that have been regarded as the decisive milestones. The study of these periods has been carried on more or less purposefully, or they have at all events been made the object of lively attention. The ethnologists, however, look upon the period after the First World War as the introduction to the present, while the real contemporary stage does not begin until the end of the Second World War.

As long as evolutionism dominated also the views of the humanists it was origins and the uniformity of the chains of development that played the leading role. After this the theory of cultural circles gave rise to a sharpened historical interest, while among British writers the somewhat older behaviourism, like social psychology in other quarters, placed the main stress upon the study of living persons. On the whole, reflections of all this are observable also in Scandinavia.

For the anthropologists it was, of course, easier to meet with primitive conditions in actual life and their field-work was therefore carried on rather undisturbed by the general development in Europe, with its undermining of tradition. The folklife researchers had to stick to more backward fringe regions and enclaves more in the nature of survivals in various localities to be able to capture communities and culture-complexes of

1

more unchanged character. I may refer to my investigation of Kila village on the border between Östergötland and Småland in 1912–13. Fifteen years later, on the occasion of a visit to the same place, the village lands had been partitioned by the land-surveying authorities, the peasants had left the district and the social milieu had become so radically changed that I was questioned by the inhabitants concerning the earlier conditions obtaining in the village as if I had been the bearer of the tradition.[1]

The more historically oriented science of ethnology is characterized by, *inter alia*, interest for the development of the living conditions and cultural changes and the dating of this development. The dating of a building, an object, a custom, a form of community, a religious conception is and has been one of our specialities. In this way we try to place the phenomena in question in their temporal context. This has been supplemented with the establishing of their localization and their social level, all of which we have referred to as the three ethnological dimensions. It is probably scarcely necessary to expatiate here on the versatility of the folklife researchers' Scandinavian inventories and their different contributions.

Here, in the 1920's, the students of folklife continued their collecting and their researches without devoting particular attention to the stratum of contemporary life. It was only in the 1930's that they began more consciously to tackle problems pertaining to the here and now.

But the folklife researchers carried on their work on different fronts. I expressed by views on this subject in an article "Folklife research in our time from a Swedish point of view" (*Gwerin*, Vol. III) in the year 1962:

> About 1950 we came to the conclusion that the great collecting phase in our country must be wound up. The reason for this was, amongst other things, that the genuine traditional material had become more and more diluted, the general social and cultural conditions had been changed in a decisive way. Our nation-wide inventories, which had already yielded good harvests, had lost their character of salvage actions.

We are not here called upon to try to follow the way in which the older French sociology gradually permeated opinion, the way in which in Britain social anthropology grew up with new manifestos and little by little also the investigation of local modern realities in various parts of the world, or how in western Europe, Germany and the U.S.A. sociology gradually began to concentrate its main interest on contemporary phenomena.

[1] Sigurd Erixon, *Kila En Östgötsk Skogsby*. En byundersökning, 1912–13, Institutet för Folklivsforskning Stockholm, Lund, 1946. Concerning the village investigations to which this work led, see also: Bebyggelseundersökningar, *Fataburen*, 1918.

In the year 1929 the American sociologist R. S. Lynd published his investigation of *Middletown*, which in 1937 was succeeded by *Middletown in Transition*, creating therewith a standard type of sociological urban community. At the same time important studies concerning "rural sociology" were organized in the U.S.A. Counterparts to these appeared also in Germany and Britain. I may mention here as an American example James West's *Plainville* (New York, 1945).

A major attack on historical orientation was launched by Bronislaw Malinowski in the 1920's and 1930's, in which connection he tilted ironically, and unjustly, of course, at the ethnologists' "fear of tackling living conditions and life-problems". According to him, they had "tried to hide behind a Chinese wall of purely antiquarian wisdom". And he was equally sceptical of the constant attempts to explain origins and developments and of the artful theories of dispersion. This very soon began to colour opinion in various quarters, including also Scandinavia, though this was more or less unconscious. At the end of the 1920's Wilhelm von Sydow began his reorientation, implying, *inter alia*, the view that the old main figures of popular belief were best explained in the light of modern psychology.

In European folklife research, too, interest in present-day problems began to increase. In Germany the term *Gegenwartsvolkskunde* was coined, and a large number of writers made contributions on the subject all over the German-speaking area. In the years 1934–5, in *Die Deutsche Volkskunde*, Adolf Spamer made contemporary man the main source for the fixing of the German people's community spirit and certain other attributes which according to the doctrine characterized this people.

In Sweden, in the year 1930, Professor Herman Geijer spoke at a meeting of folklife researchers in Gothenburg about the decay of popular tradition, and he warned his hearers against an all-too-systematic collecting of "lock, stock and barrel". However, what the speaker probably had chiefly in mind was the working methods of the Uppsala Institute for Dialectology and Folklore Research and of certain of its collaborators. He confirmed, on the other hand, what the ethnologists had hinted earlier. When, in addition to this, the same train of thought was taken up by Martin P:son Nilsson 11 years later in a lecture on the decay of popular tradition[2], he based his talk on experiences from his native district and discussed the consequences of this development. For him, the saving of the older tradition was from the scientific point of view what was most

---

[2] *Saga och Sed*, Uppsala, 1941.

important, and he suggested that the State should provide the necessary funds for an acceleration of the work of collecting.

In my article "Regional European Ethnology" in *Folkliv* 1937, I took up the notion of research on the present in the following way:

> Analyses of the present-day phase have, it is true, been carried out to a large extent, but without regard to the needs and points of view here put forward. It is thus profound and comprehensive analyses of this kind which now constitute the most pressing demand. In my opinion, however, it is not possible to realize any essential side of ethnology's aims without an extensive new orientation also in respect of the study of man. The striving must be for surer methods and more fixed systems for a comparative investigation of man.[3]

I had discussed these trains of thought in my lectures ever since the spring of 1935, and in this connection I stressed especially the necessity of taking into consideration the "three ethnological dimensions"[4] and "grouping and function" as well as, finally, "functional analysis and time studies".[5]

In the year 1938, in the handbook *Svenskt Folkliv* (Swedish Folklife), I wrote: "Since no other period than our own can be subjected to an all-round or depth analysis in the way we have here in mind, the contemporary stage has for ethnological research an importance and value beyond all other stages. It is the most reliable point of departure as regards synthesis and a whole view." In the main, I can still subscribe to this. I emphasized at that time that the aim was "to take a retrospective view, with the help of this contemporary stage (which was conceived as covering at the most a generation), of older stages". I added that "the decisive factor for the maintaining of the living connection between different stages is tradition, which must therefore occupy the focus of ethnological interest". And it is on these principles, in fact, that folklife research has on the whole been carried on up to the present. I cannot here give any bibliographic survey of the contributions of the folklife researchers up to the present, but certain observations may none the less be more definitely outlined.

In proportion as the school subject civics crystallized out and put the main stress on the present while ignoring historical information (a trend that was asserted for the first time in 1933 and more emphatically in 1946 and after),[6] several of our younger folklife students began to turn

---

[3] *Folkliv* I, 1937.

[4] *Folkliv*, 1937, p. 106.

[5] *Folkliv* II, 1938, p. 263.

[6] Cf. Birger Bromsjö, "Samhällskunskap som skolämne", Academic thesis, Stockholm, 1960.

away from the historical aspects and interest themselves more in contemporary life and its demands—despite the fact that the subject was not reckoned as one of the social sciences.

After earlier having devoted their main interest to geographical occurrences of culture elements and the routes for their dissemination, with the establishing of Sweden's cultural areas and the boundaries between them, as well as effective centres of emanation, researchers began in the twentieth century to discuss the details connected with the spreading of new departures. This applied first and foremost to matters of costume, which are sensitive to changes in fashion, and in this field Sigfrid Svensson was a pioneer. He afterwards came to devote a systematic interest to these questions and attracted followers, who in the 1940's and after threw light on innovations in costume-culture. I refer here to Sigfrid Svensson's dissertation for his doctorate on *Scania's National Costumes* (Stockholm, 1935) and to his work *Countryside and the Outer World* (Stockholm, 1942). In this latter work light was thrown on the invasions of new departures also in other fields than that of dress. The mediating breakers with tradition represented certain groups and the question became clearly socio-historical. This writer and his pupils have tried through a succession of sampling observations to show how "the novations came to the countryside", especially in South Sweden. For the rest, most of us made contributions pertaining to the dissemination of culture elements. The nature of culture was ventilated and the concept of folk-culture was isolated and distinguished. Our native centres of emanation were in most cases found to be relay stations from centres outside the frontiers of our own country. It was observed that a sort of centrifugal activity characterized the spreading of many fashions, which lost their attraction in the centre of a realm when they had reached the periphery, and so forth.

The conditions of dissemination were used as aids in combination with the work of charting. This, in the 1930's, came to play an ever greater role, especially as from 1935, when work was commenced on an atlas over Swedish folk-culture.

Also by some of those who had been inspired by von Sydow contributions to the spreading of innovations were made as from the 1940's. In the year 1947 Albert Eskeröd summarized his view of the changes in harvesting customs in Scania due to the influence of modern rationalization. Here he connected up with the view of the British social anthropologists according to Malinowski's and Radcliffe-Brown's ideas.

In the directive for the Chair of Nordic and comparative folklife research it was laid down in 1919 that all the social classes were to be studied.

This was, accordingly, applied; but there was a traditional division of labour which tended to the result that the ethnologists devoted themselves to the peasants and those working for them while the upper class was left to the art-historians. The middle class, which was rather overlooked, was studied sporadically in both quarters. Manor-houses, towns, industries and workers were, however, made subjects of interest for the students of folklife in various connections. Little by little "upper-class section" at the Nordic Museum came to a certain extent to apply also ethnological methods for the work of collecting. In Sweden this has never constituted any serious problem. Thus now, when the Nordic Museum has brought the collections together in categories according to function, this entails only certain worries for the schooling required of the officials. In general there was no discussion of the social classes at the meetings here in question. The situation abroad has been another. Professor V. E. Peuckert in Göttingen, for instance, has declined to study anything but the peasantry and the proletariat. On German soil this is in part connected with the notion of the community's split into a lower stratum and an upper stratum, the latter giving and the former only consuming. After a number of debates this notion was finally abandoned. A view opposed to Peuckert is, on the other hand, asserted by Professor Jouko Hautala, who in his *Introduction to the Fundamental Principles of Folklore Research*[7] stated the necessity for the folklorists to study all social classes in the present. Reservations against this were made by Professor Svahle Solheim, Oslo, who wanted to restrict folklore research to the old peasant community as far as the latter's view reached. I shall revert to these questions in the following.

The position and vicissitudes of the working class were early made the object of comparative historical research, but without this being reflected in the Nordic area until the twentieth century. It was after the First World War that the workers' own pioneers began to devote themselves to studies of older injustices, but at the same time also underlined the integral way in which the workers entered in the country's general development. Thus in the year 1926 the Workers' Culture-Historical Society was formed, which was given the task of dealing with the workers' life in the present and earlier, as well as with the history of the labour movement. On this occasion I gave the introductory lecture and the Nordic Museum co-operated with this Society, which also published its own periodical. An archive for the history of the labour movement was also established. In the year 1934 I gave an address at one of the jubilees of the Swedish

[7] Helsinki, 1957.

Cooperative movement on "New departures in Swedish ways of living 100 years ago", in which connection I adduced a good many facts concerning the workers' older housing conditions. I dealt with, for example, the workers' lives and conditions in a survey in 1944[8] and in the same decade. In the 1940's the Swedish Confederation of Trade Unions placed funds at disposal for a big compilation dealing with the history of the working class, and the director of the Nordic Museum, Professor Andreas Lindblom, was commissioned to edit a couple of volumes on *The Worker on Weekdays and Sundays*, which came out in 1943–4. He mobilized museum personnel to collaborate in the work and a series of questionnaires were sent out to regional informants and contacts of the trade-union movement, whereby a very rich material was brought together from which, subsequently, Mats Rehnberg published a series of autobiographical contributions devoted to the different subjects. Also other histories of the working class and contributions on the debate which arose were published. In the neighbour countries the idea was taken up by the ethnologists, and with sociological collaboration scientific technical investigations of great interest were carried out. This above all through Edvard Bull's work *Arbeidermiljø under det industrielle giennombrudd* Oslo, 1958.[9] In the main, this research may be said to have shown certain older traditions in part lingered on but began to disappear at the same time as manifold social injustices were corrected under the pro-labour régime which was generally in control. Also some monographs on manufacturing enterprises and communities were written by ethnologists. As an example of these one may mention Björn Hallerdt's *Life in a Manufacturing Community, a study in social relations at Surahammar mill 1845–1920*.[10] The sociological tendency was here very much to the fore.

In the middle of the twentieth century research on industrial workers was taken up in earnest also from ethnological points of view, at first above all by Wilhelm Brepohl.[11] In Switzerland detailed analyses of the development during the nineteenth century and also in part the twentieth were carried out by especially Richard Weiss' pupils, e.g. Rudolf Braun.[12]

[8] Cf. Sigurd Erixon, Dagligt liv i helg och söcken i Fredrikström m.fl., *Arbetets söner*, Stockholm, 1944.

[9] Oslo, 1958.

[10] Stockholm, 1957.

[11] Wilhelm Brepohl, *Der Aufbau des Ruhrvolkes im Zuge der Ost-West. Wanderung*, Dortmund, 1948. See also *Industrievolk im Wandel von der agraren Zon industrieller Daseinsform am Ruhrgebiet*, Tübingen, 1957.

[12] Cf. Rudolf Braun, *Socialer und kultureller Wandel in einem ländlichen Industriegebiet in 19. und 20. Jahrhunderten*, Zürich, 1965. Braun has also profited from Strübin, *Baselbieter Volksleven*, Basel, 1952.

Since prehistoric times the towns have been more advanced than the rural districts, above all through the specialization in different occupational groups and through the more crowded living conditions. The towns have always made their influence felt, with the result that the rural districts are beginning to become urbanized. This contrast, in combination with the dependence and influencing of the rural districts, is the drama that has especially interested British and American archeologists and anthropologists occupied with the Near East and the influences from there. In Italy and Germany the Renaissance yielded valuable histories of towns, with also ethnological elements. In Sweden, too, one later finds a number of such contributions. I will here content myself with a reminder of M. G. Craelius' brilliant description of life in Vimmerby, which is included in his *Attempts at a Description of a Province*, printed in 1774.

In the twentieth century one finds in Germany experiments with "Volkskunde" in the towns. These were at first one-sided. About 1930 a special "Gross-stadtsvolkskunde" was launched by a large number of researchers, who also deepened the subject. As regards America it must here suffice to refer to R. S. Lind's *Middletown* study, in the foreword to which Cl. Wissler remarked: "This volume needs no defense; it is put forth for what it is, a pioneer attempt to deal with a sample American community after the manner of social anthropology." It is a cross-section study of the activities in a present-day community which deals with the conditions of life, the way of forming a home, the upbringing of children, the use of leisure, the role played by religion and social functions of different kinds. Middletown was subsequently dealt with again in 1937 by the same author, with a view to the changes the town had undergone in connection with its growth and a number of cultural conflicts which arose on this account. In these studies one notes the social anthropological school, sometimes also with a specially sociological tendency.

The Swedish contributions on the field of municipal research were, as far as the ethnologists were concerned, more or less sporadic, even if an occasional paper was submitted. The Nordic Museum worked in its upperclass department with researches on buildings, studies of handicrafts and certain special investigations which were gradually intensified under the influence of the ethnologists. In art-historical circles, furthermore, a municipal research with a sociological trend was started, a couple of volumes being printed under the editorship of Professor Gregor Paulson. At the same time the Uppsala Institute for Dialectology and Folklore Research started a collection of traditional material in the Swedish towns, throwing light upon customs, usages and popular notions.

Parallel with this, manor-houses and mill-communities were dealt with as special units, even if in Sweden this research did not develop special methods or base its results on theoretical standpoints of its own.

In the year 1937[13] I advanced certain views which in 1938 I formulated to the effect that:

owing to the necessity for a restriction of activities (our) investigations have hitherto been mainly directed towards the rural population, something which has been motivated by the latter's historical significance, due to its greater exemption from outside influences and more primitive character and the decisive transformation upon the threshold of which it just now stands. But in the degree in which this has been possible the investigations have been extended to cover also other social classes, a research activity that in recent years has been consistently and constantly intensified.

This did not imply any clear line of demarcation, but on various occasions I have since pointed out that the whole populace should be subjected to our investigation, with the exception perhaps of the persons, institutions and interest-groups that direct the business of the State and scientific development and break new ground in leading subjects. In his *Civilisation Traditionelle et Genres de Vie*[14] A. Varagnac has formulated the thesis that folklore had begun to deal with every human group and culture-phenomenon that was not a product of previous scientific treatment and literary documentation.

As conditions have developed, this question has become a main issue, and I therefore take the opportunity to mark here my present view as to what should be excluded. It is a question of material which through decisions subject to control has acquired national validity and that which represents science, the official religion, the economic and technical planning which has been given literary fixation, esthetic forms approved in the central circles of the realm, social customs, general social organizations and official entertainments and sports. For the rest, the bearers of these institutions and genres should be analysed by ethnology.

In the year 1962 I wrote (in *Gwerin*):

People nowadays live and work in often completely transformed milieus constituting a network of criss-crossing relations and overlapping fields of contact. The social grouping has changed, old frontiers and barriers have begun to be effaced, the general turnover and the launching of new culture traits have been speeded up and their impingement on the individual is often of such short duration that there is no time for assimilation to folk culture before they are replaced with something else.

[13] *Folkliv*, 1937.
[14] Paris, 1948.

In a survey of the Åbo conference from 1959, to which I shall be reverting, Nils Arvid Bringéus wrote:

> It would nevertheless be incorrect to regard the cultural changes during the last hundred years as an even continuation of a process of change begun much earlier. Rather is it a question of a tremendous acceleration. The increased tempo is perhaps most clearly perceptible in the development of fashions. Whereas in former times the wheel of fashion might take decades, perhaps centuries, to go round it now revolves as rapidly as the seasons.

It is this rapidity and mutability in combination with the increased conditioning capacity of the mass media and the lack of culture barriers in the geographic sense that characterizes the present age. Social contrasts still exist, but are becoming more restricted. Innovations pour in from all quarters and the advent of a fresh novelty rather easily effaces a somewhat older one. At the same time the existence of international chain-contacts and transports between producers, middle-men and consumers, all of which affect existence and therewith also individuals, is increasingly noticed.

We have to take into consideration the material inventions and their repercussions, the economic nexuses, propaganda for ideas, advertisement and all kinds of mass media. This would imply an all-too-great load if ethnology were to try to carry everything by itself, but nowadays we have the help of economic history, technology, geography, sociology and so forth.

When, further, industrialization and the processes of urbanization have gone so far that the agrarian traditions and the old social grouping have been replaced by something new that depends upon industrial standardization, the folklife researcher has become so hemmed in that one may ask: What can and shall he do? In an article "The national atlases of folk culture" (*Folkliv*, 1960–1) I stated:

> The present is characterized by an increasingly revolutionary levelling and an ever more radical effacement of the older regional contrasts, local culture foci and frontiers. The cause is to seek in, besides the democratization of the community, the temporal neutralizing of distance and a consistently intensified central direction, the organized communication of news and a propaganda machinery of earlier unknown kind and strength. One consequence of this is that the regional culture changes have begun to plane more and more and there is a transition to general national culture. For the ethnologist this implies a significant turning point. He can no longer hold fast only to the methods and principles that have hitherto predominated in the treatment of older stages, especially if he wants to make comparative observations concerning the gradual ousting of the traditional forms under the pressure of the spreading and victorious advance of the innovations or regroupings and the changes in the roles of the different social classes in cultural life. Folklife

research cannot without thorough self-examination make contributions in this field. New methods become necessary as soon as one wishes to devote oneself to essential tasks in our own epoch. A charting with the aim of reconstruction of the kind that was applied and was required when it was a matter of the folk culture before the first World War would here miss the mark. This is at all events the conclusion at which I have arrived in the study of Swedish material.

I added that geography had now also begun to make deep and type-forming investigations on the distribution of innovations, in which connection I was thinking especially of Torsten Hägerstrand's researches in southern Östergötland, in which he wanted to free himself from the pre-destination doctrines of the older geography, based upon the notion of the dominance of natural conditions, and also from statistical superstition. He tries to reveal regularity and typical happenings in the dissemination processes and places the main stress upon centrally directed informative activities. Other geographers have dealt with, *inter alia*, receptivity for new ideas which has direct connection with different kinds of market studies.

In consideration of the aim which in the year 1938 I indicated as of importance for modern folklife research, viz. that "the analysis of the groupings, the relations and the functions in and between the groups in the contemporary stage will afford the means of being able successively to throw light also upon earlier stages", the dying of the traditions and the general mutability imply a serious crisis.

Several conferences have been held for the discussion of contemporary researches in our neighbour sciences, which have engaged themselves more purposefully than we in the enterprises started by groups for folk-studies of a social nature and for state interests. Here, however, the folklife congresses play a greater role.

At the conference on special subjects that we arranged in Saltsjöbaden in 1951 (so far published only in stencil), the relation of folklife research to the present-day stage was the subject of very lively debate. Among those who most zealously demanded that the folklife researchers should devote themselves to the present was Albert Eskeröd, who considered that better economic support should be forthcoming from the State than had hitherto been the case. Sigfrid Svensson opined that the present cannot be understood without a knowledge of tradition, and referred to Richard Weiss' so-called *Gegenwartswissenschaft*, in which despite the concentration on the present the factor of tradition played a great role. He considered that with a view to the tuition the State must see to it that the different subjects complemented each other, and the majority were agreed that sociology, which in our country wishes only to deal with the present, might supplement folklife research. I pointed out that at the Social Sciences Conference that was held in Uppsala in 1950 the historical aspects for sociology had been assigned to folklife research. I added: "we are, however, looking forward to a future development in which central direction and standardization are carried further, so that the need for a more detailed study of objects is reduced and replaced by more quantitative and physiological tasks. The whole of our science may in this way come to undergo changes implying an approach to statistically based sociology."

At the meeting for Nordic folklife and folklore research in Åbo in 1959 the spreading of innovations was taken up anew with special attention paid to the more or less individual breakers with tradition or those working to this end in groups. The introductory lecture was on this occasion held by Sigfrid Svensson, who recapitulated what had been done in Sweden in this field of research. A series of surveys were given, throwing light upon the changes in the peasant culture in different parts of Scandinavia, and in connection therewith excellent characterizations of a number of these rural milieus also during the twentieth century were given. In general there was disagreement on the question of whether it was really a matter of a dissolution of the peasant community. The majority denied this. For the concluding lecture Knut Kolsrud gave a detailed analysis of "the dissolution problem-complex in ethnology", pointing out in this connection that the word *dissolution* must imply that the whole cultural unit and its structure had been changed.

That a change in system had occurred in the social order was, however, clear. The traditional local-bound structure is in process of being changed, and the peasant now represents only a certain occupational group in the country and meets, as such, both oppositions and competition. Formerly the peasant had quite a different position.

In my contribution I asserted in 1938, as has already been indicated that tradition is the decisive factor for the maintenance of the connection between different stages, and it must accordingly occupy the focus of the ethnologists' interest. In a historical orientation on "Historismus und Präsentismus" (1954)[15] Herbert Freudenthal reckoned with "der Gegenwart" for "die Volkskunde" which he regarded as an historical science, and added that tradition (*die Überlieferung*) is "Das Wesen des Volkstums" but is independent of the "world of form". At the meeting in Åbo in 1951 Sigfrid Svensson stressed that the present cannot be understood without a knowledge of tradition. In this respect his opinion was in agreement with that of Richard Weiss, who made radical use of facts from

[15] *Beiträge zum deutschen Volks- und Altertumskunde I*, Hamburg, 1954.

present-day folklife but always maintained the demand for comparison with earlier conditions as the supporting foundation in this connection. The majority of Nordic folklife researchers have been in agreement on this point.

In the year 1966 German-speaking Volkskunde researchers and folklorists came together at a conference in Tübingen for Erforschung der Gegenwart.[16] Very different contributions were made; in one quarter it was considered that the study of the present had above all the task of comparing with the past (e.g. Karl-S. Kramer). A certain aversion was expressed here and there against the museum officials and their work, e.g. in connection with the definition of the concept folk-art. Ingeborg Weber-Kellermann, who in 1965 wrote a survey of the Grosstadtsvolkskunde research in Berlin (*Hessische Blätter*), wanted radically to change the notion of tradition, which she thought instead was due to the influence of fashion. She traced here a process of development in which certain individuals were influenced by a special social *Leitbild*, a process which did not require that this should be credible but was simply due to the fact that the persons in question wanted to follow a certain social group. A contribution by Herbert Schwett referred to the consequences of industrialization. He considered that the clergy and teachers were most frequently behind the novations. New local characters might arise, in which connection old usages might be deformed and acquire another import. The inhabitants of a marketing centre had a greater self-assurance than others and the same applied to every centrally located town and administrative locality. In a couple of lectures the role played by associations was discussed. There was a general demand for investigations that should control what had been advanced.

The Nordic researchers are in general probably divided as regards Weber Kellermann's simplified view of tradition. It is a considerably more complicated phenomenon than she reckoned with. K. Robert Wickman asserted at the Saltsjöbaden meeting in 1951, that there is a contemporary tradition as well as a tradition that we have inherited. Anna-Maja Nylén went further, and wrote in 1961, in *Tradition and the Present*: "The unconsciously received traditional material had formerly a decidedly greater compass than that which has been given verbal expression, while nowadays the literary tradition and films, radio and television of course assume greater importance as channels for tradition with every generation." It is in my opinion not suitable to confuse with these new forms the older tradition with its deeper acceptance and its greater solidity, which generally

[16] Cf. *Volksleben, Populus Revisus, Tübinger Vereinigung für Volkskunde*, 14 vols., 1966.

implies that it retained its grip for more than a generation, indeed, not infrequently remained unchanged for centuries. Neo-tradition—as I here designate for the time being the counterpart of the older tradition in the new era—is often due to the influence of fashion, to uniform central direction over the entire realm or to more adventitious influences. It is much more easily and quickly abandoned and is either a quasi-compulsive group attribute or else more individual. These different kinds of "tradition" must be seriously studied but not identified.

A British social anthropologist, Eric R. Wolf, declares in *The Social Anthropology of Complex Societies*, published in the year 1966 by M. Banton, that the degree of central direction and standardization in modern occidental communities is overestimated. This is an assertion which European ethnologists do not consider acceptable otherwise than in districts of a very special character. Scandinavia, at all events, is now traditionally undermined, and the same applies to the industrial countries in Europe. However, one's judgement will depend upon which factors one considers significant. It seems as if Wolf's opinion is based upon the social anthropological interest in quantitative changes. But it must here be pointed out that in proportion as the older social and geographical contrasts begin to be effaced and central direction increasingly determines both conditions of living and culture patterns for all milieus and strata, the possibility of basing scientific results thereon becomes less profitable.

Another of the sources of error against which systematic ethnology must be protected is the exaggeration of the role played by the quantitative factor. Even when a need exists it can be satisfied in many different ways, and often otherwise than is assumed by statistical science. This does not mean that the quantities must not be reckoned with to a certain extent in the present-day stage as in earlier stages.

Since individuals no longer themselves manufacture their products the problems of the division of labour and the role of the individual in production have become less important and now belong above all to the households and family life. What, however, is probably the most important desideratum is to try to throw light on the depth of the individual's engagement in his activities and the different forms of culture, and this also outside the sphere of practical living. To make nowadays detailed analyses of a technical nature or concerning material culture in general is hardly motivated in the absence of special causes. On the other hand, orientation and eventually also modules concerning various groups of concrete subjects are called for. These folklife research must to a certain extent take from its neighbour sciences.

It should not, however, be forgotten that peripheral and relic areas do still exist where development has earlier stagnated and where a research is rewarding both from the historical point of view and in order to show in detail how the transition takes place. But folklife research must not restrict itself to this; it must tackle in earnest the main problems which refer to modern man's conditions of existence and cultural development in the more central regions, representative for each country *per se*.

Certain groups of subjects have of old been especially cherished. This applies above all to festive usages, religious conceptions, customs and folk poetry, which for the folklorists appear as the one thing necessary. In material culture it is to building and home furnishing that since the early nineteenth century both local analyses and comparative surveys have been devoted, although these subjects in general require treatment. The same holds for costume research. The villages and industries have in certain countries been considered to lie outside folklife research, while in other countries they have been accorded a place of honour. Among the last-mentioned are the Scandinavian countries. This applies also to village organization and the social culture forms in general.

At the meeting of Nordic folklife researchers in Falun in June 1966, Poul Strømstad gave an account of "An investigation of a quarter in Copenhagen", which was further illustrated with the magnificent work *Ildebrandshuse*,[17] which work was produced by Axel Steensberg's pupils and published by the National Museum in Copenhagen in 1966. In the majority of cases the investigations have been made in buildings that had already been left by the inhabitants, but in other cases they were prevailed upon to give an account of their homes and their home life, all of which makes this rich investigation of a city quarter stand out, both through its illustrations and its text, as exemplary. However, this is not research on the present in the strictest sense of the term. Such research is, certainly, carried on here and there, but it has hitherto not so often been published as yet. Docent Sven B. Ek in Lund has recently come forward as an ardent advocate of ethnological research in contemporary population centres and towns, the emphasis being above all on the style of life and the transformation of norms, customs and habits. Under the title "On the threshold of a new attempt at a start" he has in *Folkliv* given an account of the aims and the works so far produced, all of which appears promising. The Nordic Museum and its officials have also in different ways and in

---

[17] *Ildebrandshuse. En bygningshistorisk og etnologisk undersøgelse af 24 ejendomme i gaderna Åbenrå-Landemaerket i København*, which work was carried out by Axel Steensberg's pupils and published by the National Museum in Copenhagen, 1966.

different connection contributed both investigations and theoretical pro-
nouncements. These contributions are in the main characterized by the
main stress being placed upon a present-day stage already left behind
and upon comparisons with older states and traditions. The same applies
to one of the most rewarding contributions to research on customs in the
present, Mats Rehnberg's dissertation *The Lights on the Graves* (1965).
In this, he has against the background of the history and distribution of
these customs shown with European perspective how irrespective of class
difference, residential district and social position modern people are related to these customs. A large number of questionnaries have been sent
out and also other methods of questioning have been resorted to, and the
extremely rich material of replies has been processed in statistical and
tabular form. Comparatively, the investigation concerns the whole of our
part of the world.

Also the general ethnologists came finally to realize that the primitive
cultures had suddenly begun to be transformed under European influence,
concerning which one may mention, *inter alia*, Godfrey and Monica Wil-
son's *The Analysis of Social Change. Based on observations in Central
Africa* (Cambridge, 1945). This tremendous readjustment first found expression in harbour towns and commercial centres, where the coloured
peoples came into closer contact with the foreigners. Little by little, interest for this has grown among both the social anthropologists in England
and the culture-anthropologists in the U.S.A.

As far as folklife research is concerned a concentration on contemporary
life implies a thorough ventilation of its own functions, realities and valuations on the basis of its peculiar character. It is a matter of a process
through which the actual situation of the here and now is continuously
being turned into time past. What is needed to capture this is a forward-
directed research not dependent on retrospective comparisons. One might
almost speak of an X-ray filming of the process if this were possible.

The groups of materials grow and grow with every year. What is required
is limitation and a firm setting of targets.

European ethnology has for a long time postponed taking up a definite
attitude to the new problems the structural change has thrown up in the
form of new rural and urban units, densely built-up areas and regroup-
ings of the population, removals and the setting down in new contact
groups and fields of conformity under the influence of the ever more important towns. This is a social task which also implies taking account of
the results of democratization and the new social and physical combinations that are growing up.

Here, perhaps, the British social anthropology which has survived and continued to develop since the days of Malinowski and Radcliffe-Brown may be of some use. This research puts the community problems in the first place and regards man's living and cultural conditions as dependent on these problems at the same time as they create new combinations. In general, the social anthropologists have refrained from giving any detailed account of other ethnological categories; but they do take up an attitude to economy, occupations, life-cycles and religion and discuss these according to functional viewpoints with economic, social and physiological methods developed in England, America and to some extent in France and Germany. In this connection they have been influenced by sociology. This discipline has in the main devoted its interest to the coloured peoples. During the 1950's, however, the sociologists began also to emphasize valuations, status, authority, qualifications for leadership and, finally, the structural transformation and the great mutability, with an eye to the present-day stage. But social anthropology is not purely a science of today. Especially the leading British social anthropologist E. E. Evans-Pritchard has sharply emphasized its historical character.

For the European ethnologists it is particularly interesting to note that the social anthropologists have also begun to experiment with investigations in Europe in the form of restricted village or municipal studies and studies of certain tendencies and conditions of development in the big cities. In this connection reference is generally made to W. Thomas' and F. Znaniecki's *The Polish Peasant in Europe and America* (New York, 1927) as a pioneer work, but otherwise it seems to be Irish, Welsh, Spanish and Greek communities as from the 1940's that have been of importance for this new approach. A purely English village investigation is W. M. Williams' *The Sociology of an English Village: Gosforth* (London, 1956). This is a community in north-west England which is treated in ten chapters with the following headings: The economy, The family, Some aspects of the life-cycle, Kinship, The social classes, Formal and informal associations, Neighbours, Community, Gosforth and the outside world, Religion. Here one finds the families analysed in relation to different viewpoints, above all the economic factor. Marriage and elements from the life-cycle are, moreover, dealt with statistically. Kinship is well recorded, and particular interest is devoted to the relation between the classes and different nexuses and groupings. The Spanish municipal investigation *The People of the Sierra*, published in the year 1954, by J. A. Pitt-Rivers, has a foreword by Evans-Pritchard which emphasizes as noteworthy the fact that this social-anthropological work is devoted to "our own civilization". The author himself stresses that his main concern is to show "the social structures of a rural community". Besides the vital aspects with which Williams worked, this latter study has chapters devoted to: Status and age, Political structure, Friendship and authority, Law and morality. Pitt-Rivers says that by "structure" is meant not individuals but activities and institutions. A "society" is not an "agglomeration of persons", but "a system of social relations". Besides all this it emerges that also the relation to the supernatural plays a role for status and political authority.

It is approximately these conditions that have been dealt with in certain British works such as Alwyn D. Rees *Life in a Welsh Countryside*[18] and the work *Welsh Rural Communities*.[19] These works deserve a special discussion for which there is no room in the present context.

In Germany, too, a village research with a geographical slant and with social and in part cultural aspects has latterly been undertaken. Here it must suffice to refer to Anneliese Beimborn's *Wandlungen der dörflichen Gemeinschaft im Hessischen Hinterland*.[20] I would not here draw attention to these works if they did not so closely approximate to the ethnological approach. In this connection I may also observe that American anthropology also includes monographs of this kind. I will here content myself with mentioning Manning Nash's *Machine Age Maya, The Industrialization of a Guatemalan Community*.[21]

The social consequences of technical changes and industrialization were made the subject for a congress in Chicago in 1960, the proceedings of which were printed in 1963 under the title *Industrialization and Society*. The character of these is economic and social-psychological; they are abstract and apply in part Max Weber's ideal type constructions. Economic development has in the world of technology proceeded from traditional technics to scientific knowledge. In agriculture the older type of farming has been abandoned and the trend is towards the commercial production of agricultural goods. In industry the basis is no longer manpower or animal exertion, but power-driven machines and monetary economy, and the goods produced are distributed in all directions through a network of exchanges. The work on estates or in villages has been taken

---

[18] Alwyn D. Rees, *Life in a Welsh Countryside*, Cardiff, 1950.

[19] *Welsh Rural Communities*, edited by Elwyn Davies and Alwyn D. Rees, Cardiff, 1960.

[20] Marburg, 1959, in *Marburger Geographische Schriften*, Heft 12.

[21] Manning Nash, *Machine Age Maya, The Industrialization of a Guatemalan Community*, The Anthropological Association, Memoir No. 87, Glencoe, Illinois, 1958, and divers others.

over by densely built-up areas. The result has been a structural change, both through structural differentiation and the appearance of more specialized and more independent social units. The process of differentiation varies from community to community and represents different variations on the way to modernization.

It is in a high degree a question of studies of groups and relations between individuals. An orientation on this subject is given by the social psychologist Dorwin Cartwright and the pedagogical psychologist Alvin Zander, both Americans, in their work *Group Dynamics, Research and Theory* (London, 1957), which has been referred to as "an authoritative collection and summation of theory and outstanding research findings on the leadership, functions, actions and patterns of small groups in all areas of social structure". As usual, the presentation is accompanied by statistical tables and explanatory diagrams. For European conditions this work is of more theoretical than practical interest.

In Britain, social anthropology is not always clearly distinguished from sociology. In 1964 Raymond Firth published *Essays on Social Organization and Values* (London), which has, however, a more anthropological slant and has nothing directly to do with Europe. Its table of contents may here suffice to give some notion of this author's attitude. The first part has to do with "Social organization" and contains six chapters, viz.: "Comment on dynamic 'theory' in social anthropology, Social organization and social change, Some principles of social organization, Marriage and the classificatory system of relationship, Authority and public opinion, Succession to chieftainship". In the second section, which deals with "meanings and values", there are six chapters, which deal with: "Structural and moral changes produced in modern society by scientific and technological advance, Social changes in the Western Pacific, The study of values by social anthropologists, Problems and assumptions in an anthropological study of religion, Religious belief and personal adjustment" and "An anthropological view of mysticism references". We have here in the main to do with the same groups of subjects as those earlier indicated. In Britain the theoretical discussion and the application of theory have been continued on different fronts. Here it must suffice to mention Elliott Leyton, "Conscious models and dispute regulation in an Ulster village" in *Man*, Vol. 1, no. 4, 1966, where an application of the French regional sociologist and anthropologist Claude Lévy-Strauss' idea of conscious and unconscious models is tested with the use of simple statistics.

In Norway, too, social-anthropological research has served directly as an example. However, when in the 1950's Knut Kolsrud made his investigations in North Norway and in this connection got on to the subject of transformation in the present he was influenced also by American cultural anthropology. Light was thrown on contemporary change by Gutorm Gjessing in the year 1954 in *Changing Lapps*. However, the whole of this trend, which has gradually come under the leadership of Professor F. Barth in Bergen, emerges most clearly in Robert Paine's *Coast Lapp Society*, I. *A Study of Neighbourhood in Revsbotn Fjord* (Tromsö, 1957) and II. *A Study of Economic Development and Social Values* (Tromsö, 1965). The first part is a highly interesting investigation of two different main subjects, the one "Ecological situations and cultural relations" under historical aspects as compared with present-day conditions and the other "Spatial organizations" such as "settlement, neighbourhood, village". It is found that the population in Revsbotn fjord has been bound to the sea, but that the people have since devoted themselves also to agriculture, and have therefore moved some distance inland. They progressed from seasonal transhumance between the 1650's and 1750's and after in modern times to a soil-bound life with the capital invested in the land. The majority now work both on the sea and with farming. After this the author discusses in an interesting way the spatial organization and illustrates its different types. In the second part of his work Paine deals with the period when the region began to be included in the economic system of the nation. In this connection, however, the ravages by the Germans on their retreat in the 1940's and the State's great contributions towards the economic and organizational rebuilding of the tract play a very special role. For this part of the study the author has taken a municipality by the name of Nordbotn as object. It is a very detailed investigation which throws light on above all the new conflicts of economic interest and restrictions and the opposition of the population to bureaucracy and greedy leaders. What is evaluated above all is the farmers' natural calm, but also free representative who can manage the connections with the State. The author discusses also other relation-groupings and dominating "associations" such as, for example, the Laestadian sect. He here goes into detail and sometimes even follows certain persons in their conflicts and successes. This volume is devoted exclusively to the present.

One notices that the social anthropologists have concentrated their interest above all on peripheral regions and rural districts that have been backward for a long time, when the transformations of the modern era have arrived late. These local investigations, of importance also for us ethnologists, must not lead us to forget that our science ought nevertheless to tackle in the first place more central regions of a more nationally typical character. In contradistinction to the social anthropology described, the ethnologist must demand an account of the concrete conditions of industrial and economic life and of the home, whether through direct observations, the demonstration of peculiar features or uniformity with the help of modules and models, which may eventually be able to express such aspects. One can, certainly, begin with social analyses and investigations of, for example, municipal quarters or multi-storey building complexes; but as soon as it is a matter of newly erected buildings one finds that no fully developed situation has had time to establish itself. The adults may here give the impression of being half paralysed in their social activity in contradistinction to the children and the teenagers, who are quicker in finding their contacts.

In the investigation I want here to suggest it is not necessary to base the work on all the social-anthropological constructions. It is a matter of starting individual and group studies at once. These will be comprehensive and difficult, and refer not only to conscious relations and frictions, the official enclosures of social life and other familiar nexuses, but also unconscious contact-connections and the problem of resemblance without direct contact. The study of the group-formations themselves in all directions, supplemented with remote groups and connections with training institutes, correctional institutions and communities of interest of all kinds is here a necessary prerequisite. One must also check up on the duration of the associations and their intensity, and assess their importance. In other words, it is in the first place a matter of making sampling investigations of a group, irrespective of how it is composed or situated.

One must proceed on the assumption that it is to be a matter of an intensive inquiry with a characterization of all individuals according to the principles of ethnology, of which I have given an account in my investigation in *Gwerin* 1962. It should to begin with not be a question of making a selection within the chosen group with more or less haphazard methods, the same interest must be devoted to every individual. It is necessary to bear in mind the great difficulties always entailed in examinations of individuals and the mistakes that easily arise there. After the conclusion of the investigation come the interpretation of the material and its classification in categories and groups, in which connection different principles of classification may be applied and carried out at different levels. It is here a matter of getting a clear idea of the connections, dependences, contacts and solidarities with other groups and a survey of how the connections are distributed, and whether fields of contact, community circles or groups with certain features in common and other associations are to be observed; likewise their durability or degree of fortuitousness. From the results of such a deep-probing and difficult investigation, if such an inquiry can really be made, one will get new *points d'appui* for the study of present-day people. As far as I know, nothing of this kind has hitherto been done.

The idea would be for these random samples to be supplemented with other similar ones so that the results might be processed together. This would lead to a system observation of contemporary community forms in the strict sense. The degree of reliability would depend on how long one wanted to carry on the observation. One method might be to return after an interval and then continue in suitable series.

Naturally, ethnological research ought also to be carried on by the side of this, firstly with the help of older methods, secondly on the basis of the new possibilities which would probably be opened up.

This is the drastic cure our ethnology ought to undertake if it is to be viable in the modern era and there be able to give something essential over and above the patchwork quilt of scattered observations of more or less retarded type to which the whole activity otherwise leads. The question is only how such an investigation is to be utilized and summarized. A complete picture can only be arrived at if one collects material referring to a stage whose duration it is not here necessary to decide. If one then wishes to make a further advance this will be through comparisons, and we return herewith to historical ethnology.

FUNCTIONAL THEORY IN THE LIGHT
OF TUAREG CULTURE

JOHANNES NICOLAISEN

Institute of Ethnology & Anthropology, University of Copenhagen

IN THIS paper I shall try to elucidate the value of certain functional concepts in the light of my own field material from the Tuareg. I use the term "functionalism" in the broadest possible sense, covering relatively modern methodologies which claim that culture and society must be synchronously analysed. For my starting-point I choose Tuareg kinship terminology and kinship behaviour. Kinship systems are of particular value in this context, as they form the basis of much functionalistic and structural ethnology.

We possess written historical material in the form of Arabic texts which throw light upon Tuareg culture back to the Middle Ages. Some Arab authors of this period tell us about Tuareg social and political organization, and there seems to be little doubt that the Tuareg then had true matrilineal rules of succession and inheritance.

With the exception of one minor Tuareg group living in the Ayr Mountains towards the east and mixed with Hausa people, all the Tuareg of today have a kinship terminology of the so-called Iroquois type, characterized by one particular term for cross-cousins, while parallel cousins on both sides are called "brothers" and "sisters".

Ego male will refer to his relations of ascending generations as his "fathers", "mothers", or "mother's brothers", while kinsmen of descending generations are called "children" or "sister's children". The classificatory use of these latter terms may vary somewhat from one Tuareg group to the other, but there is no need to give an elaborate account of this. What I wish to underline is that persons known by one and the same kinship term are not always socially equivalent, and that one particular kin term does not necessarily correspond to a definite type of behaviour. Thus Ego may address some of his classificatory fathers by their proper names, but he must say "father" when addressing his true biological father. Again, classificatory fathers do not have exactly the same kind of authority over their classificatory son, and none of them possesses authority to the same degree as the true father. Furthermore, the relationship between classificatory fathers and their "son" corresponds in many respects with the relationship between this person and his classificatory mother's brothers. Among the Ahaggar Tuareg, classificatory mother's brothers comprise all men of ascending generations matrilineally related to Ego plus all the mother's first cousins whether these are directly related to Ego in the maternal line or not. Some classificatory mother's brothers are not socially equivalent to true mother's brothers, after whom the Ahaggar Tuareg acquire rights of succession. These few examples chosen from the Tuareg of Ahaggar are sufficient indication that the study of kinship terminology does not yield any true picture of kinship behaviour: terminology and behaviour do not correspond entirely with one another. This might be illustrated by many other examples. I will adduce only one.

The Tuareg cousin terminology of Iroquois type may seem to be structured for cross-cousin marriage. Traditionally, this type of marriage is also preferred among the Ahaggar Tuareg, and it seems as if the contraction of such marriages is stimulated by certain traditions and myths and in particular by an institutional joking relationship between cross-cousins. This joking relationship between cross-cousins creates intimate contact—also sexually—between male and female cross-cousins, while the relationship between parallel cousins (classificatory brothers and sisters) does not make such contact easy because of a "respect" relationship very similar to that existing towards kinsmen of ascending generations. Among the Tuareg, younger brothers/sisters must pay respect to older brothers/sisters, and this holds also for classificatory brothers and sisters.

Though the structure of kinship terminology would seem to be fitted for cross-cousin marriage, there is no ban on marriage between parallel cousins. In fact, marriage to a mother's sister's daughter (a classificatory sister) or a mother's sister's daughter's daughter (a classificatory sister's daughter) are considered the best type of marriage by many Tuareg of Ahaggar.

As far as we know, Tuareg social organization was once pronounced matrilineal in the sense that a man had rights of inheritance as well as rights of succession after his mother's brother. Conditions today are different, as both matrilineal and patrilineal traits are prevalent. Thus the Ahaggar Tuareg have still preserved matrilineal succession to chieftainship and the like, while they have adopted Koranic inheritance rules according to which a person can inherit patrilineal kinsmen only—with the exception of inheritance rights at the death of the true mother or the mother's mother. Residence today may perhaps be described as patri/matrilo-

cal: the newly married couple stay one year in the bride's family camp
and then move to the camp of the husband's father. When the husband's
father dies the couple move to the husband's maternal kinsmen and ideally to his mother's brother. The children of the marriage ultimately belong to their mother's family and tribe. Structurally, this seemingly complex type of residence, as well as the system of inheritance and succession,
may seem to be in harmony with cross-cousin marriage. Ideal marriage patterns, however, are not always followed by the Tuareg, and this is true
particularly of second marriages. The Tuareg have a high rate of divorce
and when a man divorces to marry again his marriage may be less determined by ideal rules than his first marriage, which may have been arranged by his parents—in particular by his father. A second marriage is
not generally arranged by the parents, and a man may then very well
marry a woman belonging to another tribe. In consequence of this some
Tuareg claim that first marriages to matrilineal kinswomen may prove
more suitable than unions between cross-cousins. I do not wish to elaborate more on this, except to repeat that the traditional type of prefer-
ential cross-cousin marriage seems to be less followed nowadays than marriage to a mother's sister's daughter (termed sister) or her daughter
(termed sister's daughter). Kinship terminology is not entirely con-
sistent with the present rules of marriage. One is allowed to marry a
classificatory sister and a classificatory sister's daughter, though one may
never marry a true sister or a true sister's daughter.

It seems as if patrilineal influence from the Arabs and from Islamic
society has been important in creating new patterns for Tuareg social
organization. One might perhaps expect that a complete change to patrilinity of the Arab type would give rise to a change of kinship terminology
and behaviour as well as to changes in certain social institutions. However, such a complete change cannot be observed among the Niger Tuareg,
who with respect to rules of residence, inheritance and succession have a
type of social structure resembling that of the Arab Bedouin. Not only
Tuareg oral traditions, but also written Arab sources tell us that "pure"
patrilinity was finally introduced among the Niger Tuareg around the
middle of the seventeenth century, or towards its end. Patrilineal succession
was then adopted, while Koranic inheritance rules were probably introduced before that date. On the whole, it seems as if the Niger Tuareg have
had a patrilineal type of social organization for about 300 years, and it
would be interesting to study kinship terminology, kinship behaviour and
social institutions in the light of the change from one type of social organization to the other. I have recently been able to carry out such a study

among certain Niger Tuareg with the following results:

1. Among the Niger Tuareg there are two different systems of kinship terminology. Both have Iroquois cousin terminology and they are not very different from one another. I am unable to explain the minor differences between the two systems, one of which is completely identical with the kinship terminology of the Ahaggar Tuareg.

2. Kinship behaviour among the Niger Tuareg corresponds largely to kinship behaviour in Ahaggar. No remarkable distinction can be observed.

3. Marriage was the most important institution studied. The Niger Tuareg, like the Tuareg of Ahaggar, permit all types of cousin marriages. Marriage to a cross-cousin is common also in the Niger area where cross-cousins joke as in Ahaggar. Cross-cousin marriage is frequently described as "sweet" and is regarded as the best type of marriage by some Tuareg because husband and wife, being each others' cross-cousins, are said to live gaily and peacefully as a married couple. Marriage with a mother's sister's daughter is frequent, though said to be of no particular importance. The Niger Tuareg say that respect between matrilateral parallel cousins is less pronounced than between patrilateral parallel cousins. Marriage to a father's brother's daughter is described as being both "difficult" and "strong". This type of marriage seems to be considered the ideal by most Tuareg and fairly many marriages of this type are contracted, as may be seen from the list below.

Marriage types among the Niger Tuareg	Number of first marriages
Father's brother's daughter	17
Mother's sister's daughter	13
Mother's brother's daughter	11
Father's sister's daughter	7
Classificatory cross-cousins	5
Other kinswomen or non-related women	22
Marriages in total	75

My study of kinship and social organization among the Tuareg of Ahaggar and Niger may perhaps allow me to draw the following conclusion:

Tuareg kinship terminology and kinship behaviour seem to be structured for cross-cousin marriage, and this is further underlined by myths, traditions and certain marriage rites performed in Ahaggar. It may also be that cross-cousin marriage—marriage to a mother's brother's daughter—has an important function in solidifying the matrilineal principle by the creation of a closer relationship between mother's brother and sister's son. In Ahaggar it would seem possible to relate ideally certain traits of the kinship system to other traits of social structure, including rules of inheritance, succession, and marital residence. However, traditional social structure is apparently changing. This may perhaps be due to influence from the patrilineal Arabs and Islam, but I have not been able to analyse in detail and fully understand the process of social change which is now taking place in Ahaggar. It seems easier to deal with the Niger Tuareg. Among these Tuareg, kinship terminology and behaviour is of Ahaggar type, while social organization is characterized by "pure" patrilinity stressing patrilocal residence, patrilineal rules of inheritance and succession. At the same time patrilateral, parallel cousin marriage is considered the ideal marriage type. The social organization of the Niger Tuareg may seem to be evolving towards the Arab type of social structure, and it may be that the preferred marriage to a father's brother's daughter should be understood in terms of structural change of rules of inheritance, succession and marital residence. However, I do not think that this is the whole explanation. It seems as if the Niger Tuareg are gradually taking over the whole social structure of the Arabs as a result of diffusion. Marriage to a father's brother's daughter is now considered an ideal by the Niger Tuareg, not so much because it fits their rules of residence, inheritance, and succession but mainly because this type of marriage is considered an ideal according to the divine rules of Islamic religion.

We may perhaps claim—in agreement with other scholars—that social process can be arranged in two main categories. (1) A recurrent process linked with structure which can be understood in the light of synchronous analysis. (2) A process creating structural change to be studied diachronically. In the light of my Tuareg material I would say that social process of the latter type is at least very slow, and that social organization among the Tuareg cannot be fully understood if we do not take into account the cultural contact with Arabs and Islamic society. If this is true, diffusion is still extremely valuable as a methodological concept.

APPLIED ETHNOLOGY AS AN EXAMPLE OF ETHNOLOGICAL RESEARCH ON THE PRESENT

GEORGE NELLEMANN

Dansk Folke Museum, Copenhagen

IN RESPONSE to Professor Erixon's appeal for contributions from ethnologists who also work outside of Europe, I shall permit myself to introduce the concept *applied ethnology* into the debate and give an example from my own work.

Applied ethnology is probably the most "modern" branch of ethnology and the one which above all must work with the observation of the present. And whereas in this symposium the notion of *the present* has been defined as a period dating from today back to the First World War, to the advent of industrialization or to the earliest recollections of persons now living, the notion of the present in applied ethnology is rather a period beginning a few years ago and extending some years into the future. Applied ethnology is in the nature of things, not historically orientated, but its results will become historical source-writings of very high value.

As the majority of the participating in this symposium are researchers who are working with Scandinavian ethnology on an historical basis and who are therefore scarcely very familiar with the concept applied ethnology, which is more particularly connected with colonial administration and aid to underdeveloped countries, I will give an example of an applied-ethnological investigation and take an investigation in which I myself have taken part. I do this because, naturally, I know this investigation better than others, and also because it touches upon problems which rather correspond to the problems we encounter in the Scandinavian countries and which it is no remote notion for ethnologists to study.

The investigation was undertaken in West Greenland in 1957–8 for the Committee for Sociological Research in Greenland, and its programme was: "Why did things turn out so badly for the group of families that was moved from the Upernavik District in northernmost Greenland to the Diskobugt District farther south?" It was thus a matter of a situation which in applied ethnology is unfortunately of general occurrence:

things have gone wrong and only afterwards are we interested in asking why. The ideal would be for an investigation to be undertaken before a project is launched, so that it might show the difficulties which the project will meet with and eventually indicate how these may best be overcome or circumvented. It is thus a matter of using ethnology—in the light of what is known of the cultures involved and in studies undertaken with ethnological methods—in the service of practical life, of "applying" it to a practical object.

I shall not go into the details of the investigation and its results, but refer to the public report in Danish with abstracts in English and Greenlandic. The main result may be summarized as follows:

It was a question of moving a group of Greenlandic families within Greenland, procuring new dwellings for them, starting them off with an occupation and having them absorbed in the community to which they were moved.

Many difficulties overtook the project—impediments due to epidemics, fire in the houses to which the families had been moved and epidemics in the localities to which they were sent. These things could, of course, not be foreseen. Further, there were among the families many who were not able to work, who were obliged to live on public assistance in one form or another. At the same time, however, there were also many families that were apparently well qualified to manage but did not—it was especially these families that were investigated.

Before I go on to the results of the investigation I will say a few words about the method of investigation and a little about my own position in this community. I was sojourning, before the "Committee for Sociological Research" (Udvalget for Samfundsforskning) began the investigations in the field, in a West Greenland town where I was studying the old culture, i.e. making notes of traditions, and also had various salaried jobs to pay my way—the same applied to my wife. As before I left Denmark it was planned that I should later join the Committee's fieldwork, the central administration in Greenland got me a job as secretary in the local judiciary, whose functioning it was, amongst other things, the Committee's task to study. Besides this I had some teaching in the school and for a period I was a clerk at the electricity works, while my wife was employed in the technical section of the administration. These jobs put us in positions from which we could undertake part-time observation of certain—not unessential—aspects of the daily life.

My work of taking notes of traditions happened to be precisely in the group of transferred families the investigation came to cover. I went to these families every day and they came to us—and the contact and confidence we gained in this way benefited the subsequent investigations, just as our work in the public service made us familiar with the local archives and accounts, which was later to be of value in connection with the collection of information concerning the situation of the transferred persons in 1957–9.

The investigation consisted in charting the actual circumstances of the transferred families: their income and their expenditure, their working conditions and housing conditions, and not least their relations with the old population in the district and the authorities.

The transferred families may be roughly divided into four groups: (1) those who had already left the locality and returned home; (2) those who on account of age and invalidity were living chiefly on public assistance; (3) those who were trying to support themselves as fishermen and seal-hunters; and (4) those who were trying to support themselves as wage-earners.

As regards group (1) we may conclude that their expectations were not realized, and the group appears to have consisted chiefly of seal-hunting families. Group (2) could certainly have lived a more comfortable life in Upernavik in the milieu familiar to them and their presence in the district probably helped to lower the status of the whole of the transferred population—unproductive as it was. This group's assimilation problems were on the whole the same as for the groups (3) and (4), but no explanation is needed for its not managing economically.

The most interesting groups are thus (3) and (4), because they apparently had the possibility of managing, but in the majority of cases nevertheless did not.

Concerning group (3)—those who expected and were expected to manage as independent fishermen or seal-hunters—we may conclude that it was certainly a matter of a transfer of Greenlanders within Greenland, but also of a *long-distance removal* from one occupational geographic zone to another, a matter of a removal from—one may almost say—an "Eskimo" community to a "modern Greenlandic" one.

The transferred persons had *no knowledge of the fishing technique* that was used in the new locality, and, moreover, their view of fishing was characterized by *the Eskimo system of values:* seal-hunting is the only occupation for men, fishing is a sideline that is pursued by women, children and men who are not fit for anything else. Against this background it is not hard to understand that the desire to start the new and despised occupation was not great.

Seal-hunting in the new locality was less extensive than in the old place, and there was the further difficulty that the hunters *did not know the geography of the new region* and its possibilities. This not only lessened the yield from seal-hunting, it also apparently implied *actual security risks*. It was at all events the general view that a number of accidents were due to ignorance of dangerous places on the ice—three transferred hunters had lost their lives in ice accidents.

For those who in spite of all chose to earn a livelihood as fishermen there was the further complication that some of the families were on account of impediments due to epidemic *moved at an unfavourable time in the occupation's annual rotation*. They reached the new locality so late in the latter part of the year that they did not have time to fish for dog-food— or in any case to dry the fish they caught. As a result, their dogs died of starvation before the winter fishing started in earnest. And the winter-fishing from the ice requires a proper dog-team.

Group (4), paid work, which was also the alternative for those who did not manage to earn a livelihood as fishers and hunters, came up against the not inconsiderable difficulty that in the districts to which they were transferred there was *winter* unemployment already before their arrival. There were casual jobs going, but as a newcomer it was not easy to be considered. And here we meet with one of the most important problems in connection with a population transfer: the competition between the old inhabitants and the newcomers. If people move to districts where there is *competition for limited goods*, they are generally the losers in the competition. The old population of the locality have ways of *monopolizing the paid work* for themselves; the foremen who engage casual labour are members of the old population, and give much weight to considerations of friendship, kinship and possibly also local political conditions.

The assimilation, the actual process of assimilation, when a new population-group comes to a locality, is a process in two directions: (1) the newcomers must adapt themselves to the locality; (2) the old inhabitants of the locality must adapt themselves to the newcomers. The prerequisites for such an assimilation were the least possible. For the competition for the benefits was not limited to the paid work, but included also *dwellings* and access to *public aid* in emergencies.

Here the government regulations came to the aid of the transferred persons, since as a part of the policy of population-concentration pursued by the Danish and the Greenlandic administration the newcomers enjoy priority rights when supporting loans for housing are granted. Also as regards public assistance, there are special regulations intended to help the transferred persons to get a start in the new locality. But unfortunately it was not known to the old population that these contributions were administered quite outside of the general social assistance—the old inhabitants got the impression that the newcomers were getting contributions at their expense.

The tensions arising between the groups on account of the competition found a vent in chicanery and discrimination—something which it was difficult to get to the bottom of, but of which we managed to get to know quite a lot by observing the everyday life in the town and the administration and through the confidence attained before the beginning of the investigation.

What the newcomers were exposed to was, for example, careless attending to matters having to do with justified public assistance (invalid pension and advance payment of maintenance contributions), under-payment for private work for the old and rich families of the town, chicanery at the fisheries and towards the children in the school.

Also the municipal settlement committee did what it could further to obstruct the assimilation between the groups. Despite proposals from the Danish members of the committee, the committee would not have the newcomers living in the town itself, but referred them to dwellings outside. And in the choice of the type of dwelling for the transferred persons another mistake was made: they were given houses that did not correspond to their dwelling habits, and that were, moreover, very expensive, as regards both repayments and heating. The houses therefore fell into disrepair, the quarter allotted to the newcomers became a pronounced slum quarter—which further helped to lower the social position of the tenants.

This example of "applied ethnology" should be sufficient to show what the concept covers, what working methods must be used in a study of the present of this kind and that it is something that concerns Scandinavian ethnologists—the problems arising will be found in most studies of reorganization, urbanization and mechanization.

The experience gained may be used in the planning of other population removals—this is the sense of this kind of studies, and it is this orientation towards the future that justifies my statement that the present is not only the last of the past but also the first of the future.

Someone may perhaps say that the investigation I have described has not much to do with ethnology, or at least that much of it is occupied with problems normally belonging to other social sciences, and it is true that elementary occupational geographic, economic and sociological aspects are included in the investigation. But to this it may be answered that in the first place the disciplines referred to were not represented in the investigation, and in the second place that today there is probably no one who wants to draw sharp and narrow limits between the social sciences. As regards the method, observation and participation, there is no doubt—it is ethnological.

We are accustomed, I suppose, to investigations of urbanization processes and reorganizations of large towns being undertaken by sociologists, when we abstract from building and housing investigations—but I do not think that the results of this type of investigation will become less if the ethnologists undertake, for example, studies of the life patterns and systems of values of the population group in question, for instance as an extension of the investigations of the housing and diet habits already being carried out.

Engagement in such research on the present would mean that in a higher degree than has hitherto been the case the Scandinavian ethnologists must adopt the method which is used by colleagues who work among foreign ethnic groups: direct observation—preferably participant observation (in so far as this is at all feasible and not merely an ideal).

Such studies would, as has already been mentioned, also become valuable sources for historical ethnology, inasmuch as they would contain a lot of information that the ethnologists of the future would otherwise be obliged to try to reconstruct on the strength of the selective recollections of others and of what the archives might happen to contain.

THE TRADITIONAL SEX ROLES IN A
CHANGING SOCIAL STRUCTURE

ANNA-BRITTA HELLBOM

The National Museum of Ethnographi, Stockholm

THE import of the concepts "status" and "role" has varied in both the scientific and the general debate.[1] In particular the term "sex-role" has provoked vehement exchanges of opinion and often given rise to misunderstandings which might perhaps have been avoided through a clearer terminology based on an unequivocal import. This is an attempt to fix the import of the concept and to test its application in a specific material.

If one proceeds on the assumption that by status is meant the individual's position in a social system and that the roles are the ways in which status is expressed, together with the expectations ensuing for the statusholder, one may with reason ask: what status does the sex-role express?

In my opinion it ought only to be an expression for certain of the statuses allotted to or acquired by the individual, viz. the statuses which cannot be held by individuals of the opposite sex. These statuses I will call "biological statuses".

The intention is here to show the gradual shifting of the concept sexrole from its proper import of expression for the individual's biological statuses, i.e. certain mainly primary and allotted statuses, to become an expression also for and above all for these secondary or acquired statuses.

One can distinguish three different categories of status: (1) biological status; (2) age status; (3) other or occupational statuses. (1) and (2) I count as allotted statuses, since the prerequisite for them is the individual's sex; [2] (3) refers to acquired statuses. All of these three status-categories are naturally expressed through their respective roles.

Since the development of these roles must be seen against the background of the whole culture from which the respective statusholders take the material for their respective modes of expression this cultural background

---

[1] Cf. Goodenough (1965) pp. 1–2; Hellbom (1967) pp. 159, 279.

[2] Age-status belongs properly to the first-mentioned category, but in this connection I have preferred to separate them. Their respective roles will for practical reasons not be dealt with here nor will certain hereditary statuses and roles allotted to the individual sometimes right from birth.

should first be outlined.[3] Since, however, I shall here be dealing only with the "biological status-roles" or the sex-roles, I have chosen another descriptive mode, which in my opinion adequately meets the demand for culture-background, viz. the life-cycle. The material for exemplification is taken from present-day Mexican Indian and Mestizo culture.[4]

The life-cycle—a human being's course of life from birth, to death—covers the following periods, whose transitions are marked by certain ceremonies *rites de-passage* and during which the individual attains different statuses (see Table 1).

TABLE 1

Period	Rites-de-passage	Age-status		Biol. status (see schema "Biological status and sex-roles")	Other status
		Masc.	Fem.		
INFANCIA 0–2, 3 years	Birth, baptism/naming	*criatura*	*criatura*		
NINEZ 2–12,15 years 12–15 years 12–18 years	schooling 6–12, 15 years	*niño* *muchacho piltontle*	*niña sisigwa muchacha*		
ADOLESCENCIA 15–marriage 18–marriage	Celebration of 15th birthday	*joven telpokath*	*señorita*		
EDAD ADULTA marriage– 1 or 2 children VEJEZ –death	Wedding Burial	*hombre* *viejo anciano*	*mujer* *vieja anciana*		

The individual's other biological status, i.e. family status, accrues from childhood/birth and follows throughout life, while other statuses, e.g. occupational status, are not attained until the end of the period of youth and the beginning of the adult age-period.

[3] The description of the cultural background which is here applicable is to be found in the author's work, *La Participación Cultural de las Mujeres*, Stockholm, 1967, where also detailed source-data are indicated.

[4] The statements are taken from works by Oscar Lewis (1940's), William Madsen and R. van Zantwijk (1950's), and are to a large extent in agreement with the author's own field-observations (1960's).

LIFE-CYCLE

Infancia: 0–2, 3 years

The age of infancy varies, but in general it is reckoned from birth to 2 to 3 years. The child is called criature irrespective of sex.

Navel-string and placenta are treated ceremonially.

A name-giving ceremony is held by the midwife already at birth, and the members of the family drink the health of the newborn child.

During the first months the infant scarcely leaves the mother, in order not to get cold. Infants also run a special risk of being influenced by "the evil eye" and *"los aires"*.

Toilet-training begins only at the age of 2–3 years in certain quarters, elsewhere as soon as the child begins to walk. It ought then at the age of 3 years to be able to go to the back yard or the like and manage by itself.

Niñez: pre-school age 2, 3–7; schoolchildren 6–12, 15–18

In general the tiny tots—*niños pequeños*—live in great freedom and play under the supervision of the mother or an older sister.

Their games and their eventual toys are uncomplicated. The games begin increasingly to imitate the activities of the bigger children and, later on, of the adults.

As regards contacts with the world about them they must begin to discipline themselves early, and before their schooling begins they have had to learn not to smile at strangers for fear of the "evil eye".

Schooling

The schooling is obligatory, begins at the age of 6 years, but many begin already at 4 in the kindergarten where such an institution exists.

Participation in the school tuition is often dependent on the parents' attitude to the necessity of this. The attitudes of the parents is often connected with their need of the child's labour. Attendance tends to fall off especially during the third and fourth school-year. The falling off is at a maximum in the highest classes.

Apart from the regular school subjects the children must learn the elements of hygiene, diet and manners.

Roughly at the ages 9–12 years there is a spontaneous division according to sex, so that boys and girls play in groups and separately.

Adolescencia: 15, 18 years–marriage

The period of youth implies for the individual work in the home, which means greater respect in the family circle but not yet complete emancipation from parental authority.

Only a minority who have been able to study outside the home-village are able to improve their way of living and act as a model for their own generation. In this way is aroused a desire to improve their existence with modern clothes, shoes, bed-clothes, etc., and to see more of the world outside the home-village.

A large part of the period of youth is devoted to "courtship", something that scarcely occurred formerly on account of the girls' early marriage-age.

Nowadays the young people have greater possibilities of meeting, thanks to, *inter alia*, the schooling. To be engaged is now so common that even the Church has eased the restrictions formerly imposed and no longer considers this to be a sin.

There still remains, however, much shyness and stealth in connection with the meetings and dates, which must be without the knowledge of others, especially the parents.

Sexual relations ensue in the majority of cases, although the ideology prescribes virginity for both sexes.

Formerly, an engagement implied that the parties concerned intended to marry, but it has become increasingly the tendency for the young people to have several different partners before they marry—sometimes even simultaneously.

Edad adulta: marriage–

In general, marriage implies the entrance of the individual into the adult world, with its responsibilities and obligations, but also its higher position, its authority and better possibilities of activating.

The age for the transition from childhood and youth to adulthood has been moved up the scale, so that especially the formerly very low marriage-age for the women was moved after the Revolution to about 17–20 years. There is, however, a tendency for it to sink by some years.

Ménage in free "liaisons" became common during the revolutionary era.

Many such free liaisons take the form of "second marriages", inasmuch as the first marriage partner is still alive and according to Roman Catholic practice constitutes an obstacle to a new marriage.

The registry-office marriage is considered the most important, as it is not followed by a Church wedding. A registry-office wedding is the consequence of an abduction.

As has been mentioned, the attainment of adult age opens the door for the individual to a number of new activities over and above the primary occupational activity, some of these more or less adventitious, others more permanent. A medical man may be elected as burgomaster in the political sector, a merchant acts as *mayordomo* in the ideological sector or a housewife is employed as *curandera*, etc.

Vejez:

For many, old age implies inactivity and dependence on others, if the forces of the individuals in question do not enable them to support themselves. The majority go on working as long as they can.

Formerly, old age implied superiority and greater respect, but these attitudes are beginning to be replaced by others, something which is due to the many new situations, which give rise to conflicts between the young and the older generation.

However, old age entails greater freedom with regard to conduct and behaviour, so that certain deviations and irregularities are tolerated.

THE MASCULINE LIFE-CYCLE

Infancia: 0–2 years

The umbilical cord of a new-born boy is buried under a maguey, so that he shall become a good worker, or under a tree up in the mountains, so that he shall never be afraid of wandering in mountainous regions.

The family drinks the health of the newborn with the words: "Let us drink a toast for the woodcutter who has come to us..."

Little boys do not need to be disciplined so severely or so early as the girls in the matter of toilet-training.

Niñez: 2–12, 18 years

When the small boys play at being "daddy, mummy, child" they pretend to work in the field or fetch wood, or to make tools, etc., for the home.

Schooling

The number of enrolled boys and boys continuing their schooling is in general greater than the corresponding number of girls. The boys seem to be more inclined to play truant.

They have greater freedom to play, but it is considered desirable that they shall remain as much as possible within the pale of the home in order to avoid bad company.

Right up to the age of 17–18 years the boys are addressed with the terms for children, *muchachos* or *piltontle*, despite the fact that the period of childhood is considered to end at the age of about 14 years.

Adolescencia: 17, 18–marriage

The period of youth is reckoned from about 17–18 years, when the boys are called *jóvenes, muchachos* or *telpokath.*

The modern era shows its influence on the young people in their desire for, for example, money for sport, leisure and the possibility of visiting the towns.

Edad adulta: marriage –

Also for the men the marriage-age tends to be lowered; there are married men of 15–16 years. However, the commonest age is about 20, but also later ages, e.g. 30 and 40, occur.

It is the parents of the fiancé who formally ask the hand of the fiancée at the son's request. When he has been accepted by the girl's parents the latter inform him of his maintenance duties but also concerning the daughter's eventual faults and shortcomings.

In general a youth avoids marrying a girl who is more educated or well-to-do than he is himself, this to avoid conflicts between her and his family.

Adult life implies for the man a great variety of activities, but also responsibility and privileges.

Apart from his regular occupation and his responsibility as a breadwinner he has the possibility of acting in different cultural sectors, e.g. as *mayordomo* and *capitán* at village feasts, as a teacher, doctor, etc.

Vejez:

For the old men there are few possibilities of working at their regular occupation, as this is often agriculture, and their strength is no longer sufficient for this heavy work. In many cases they then become dependent on their children or wife.

THE FEMININE LIFE-CYCLE

Infancia: 0–2 years

The umbilical cord of the newborn girl is buried under the metate, so that she shall become a diligent grinder of maize and a good housewife.

When a girl is baptized the family drink her health with the words: "For the grinder of maize who has come to us..."

As a rule, the discipline with respect to toilet-training is a good deal harder for the girls; they must begin earlier, are more severely punished in case of failures and are expected to manage by themselves earlier.

Niñez: 2–12 years

When at the age of 2–5 years the children begin to imitate the adults in their games, the girls in the "daddy–mummy–child" games pretend to cook food, slap tortillas, boil rice and beans and look after their dolls.

Schooling

In general, the number of enrolled girls is less than that for the boys.

As regards the tuition in hygiene and the like the girls seem to learn better, to judge from their better application of the knowledge imparted.

For the girls, school implies freedom from many household chores, apart from the maternal supervision, and the possibility of making social contacts. They can make friends with other girls and meet boys.

Adolescencia: (12) 15–marriage

The period between childhood and adulthood, the age of youth, was formerly very short or was entirely lacking for the girls. In consequence of the low marriage-age they often went directly from the child stage into marriage, from *niña* to *señora*, thus skipping *señorita or ichpokame*.

Nowadays the *niña*-period has been prolonged to 15 years, after which the girls are *señoritas* up to about 20 years of age. The festive celebration of the girl's fifteenth birthday occurs mostly in mestizo and urban circles.

Marriage

The marriage-age, which was formerly very low for the women— sometimes even in pre-puberty—was raised after the Revolution to higher ages. Many girls postpone their marriage in order to get training as, for example, teachers. However, the marriage-age shows a tendency to sink again (14–15 years).

After the ceremonial courting the parents inform the daughter of her new life as a married woman and of her general obligations.

The night before the wedding is spent by the bride in the home of the godmother.

After a church-wedding and the reception in the home of the god-parents the bride is taken home to the bridegroom.

An abducted fiancée is taken to the fiancé's relatives or to his parents.

If the girl's parents after some days consent to the marriage the wedding is arranged. If not, the contacts are broken off, sometimes for a long period.

Many widows prefer to live in a free liaison rather than to remarry if the stepfather is unkind to their children. Moreover, the wives have often promised their dying husband not to remarry, precisely for this reason.

As a rule the girls try to marry richer and more educated boys. However, the fear of remaining unmarried may induce a wealthy girl who is approaching the age of 30 to marry a poor man.

Edad adulta: (marriage) 1 or 2 children–

The practical life of the adult woman implies activities in principle within the economic sector, i.e. as housewife, which means preparing food, cleaning and the care and upbringing of the children.

Apart from the traditional household chores, she may devote herself to the cultivation of vegetables and flowers, the raising of poultry and pigs, etc., and may sell her own produce at the market.

She may also do trade in homecraft products, e.g. textiles, but also other industrial products.

A more educated woman works as a teacher, chemist, nurse, midwife and curandera.

Vejez:

As a rule, many women carry on with their usual household duties when they become old. Many, especially widows, may also undertake various economically profitable tasks such as laundering, the cultivation of vegetables and fruit, and poultry raising. Others work as midwives or curanderas.

Consequently, the old women become more and more independent, both economically and emotionally, after they have completed their traditional obligations as mothers and wives.

THE SEX-ROLES

In order to avoid repetitions and an unnecessary extension of the text I will here deal only with the sex-roles which express certain biological statuses, viz. the kinship-roles, both those referring to blood relationship and those referring to in-law relationships. Certain less important roles have for the same reason been omitted except for the terms. As regards these and the age-roles, I must therefore refer to the respective life-cycles, where the statuses in question will be found under the relevant periods.

The difficulty of keeping strictly to chronological order in the description of the sex-roles is seen at once in the accounts of the kinship-roles: an individual becomes a son or daughter with his or her birth, but scarcely a parent until the age of "adulthood" is attained. Similarly, the daughter-role may be retained to an advanced age despite the individual's changed civil status, but it may also come to an end at a tender age. The strict adherence to chronological order parallel with the periods of the life-cycle is thus more fictive than realistic (see Table 2).

TABLE 2

Life-cycle	Biological status and sex-roles			
	Age status		Kinship status	
Age periods	Masc.	Fem.	Masc.	Fem.
Infancia: 0–2	*criatura*	*criatura*		
Niñez: 2–12, 15	*niño*	*niña, sisigwa*	*hijo*	*hija*
			hermano (mayor)	*hermana (mayor)*
			hijastro	*hijastra*
			sobrino	*sobrina*
			nieto	*nieta*
			primo hermano	*prima hermana*
			ahijado	*ahijada*
12–15	*muchacho,*	*muchacha*		
12–18	*piltontle*			
Adolescencia:				
15–marriage	*joven,*	*señorita*		
18–marriage	*telpokath*		*novio*	*novia*
Edad adulta·				
marriage–	*adulto*		*marido*	*mujer, esposa*
	hombre			
marriage–1 or		*mujer*	*padre*	*madre*
2 children			*padrastro*	*madrastra*
			tio	*tia*
			yerno	*nuera*
			cuñado	*cuñada*
			padrino	*madrina*
			compadre	*comadre*
Vejez	*viejo*	*vieja*	*suegro*	*suegra*
			viudo	*viuda*
			abuelo	*abuela*
			bisabuelo	*bisabuela*
			tatarabuelo	*tatarabuela*

Infancia:

criatura 0–2, 3 years (see Life-cycle).

Niñez:

niño 2–12; *muchacho, pilontle* 12–18 (see Life-cycle).

hijo (son). The youngest and the eldest son are often the mother's favourites. When the father dies the eldest son often takes over the duties as bread-winner also for the mother, which may sometimes give rise to conflicts between them.

hermano (brother). The eldest brother demands respect and obedience from the younger sibs. If the parents are dead, he undertakes the upbringing of his smaller brothers and sisters, and even as adults the latter often continue to consult the eldest brother.

primo hermano (cousin). The relationship between cousins is maintained through regular visits and reciprocal help. There are no taboos between cousins, and a boy's first sexual contact with the opposite sex is often precisely with some older cousin.

hijastro (stepson).

sobrino (brother's/sister's son). A brother's son must show respect for his uncle and also help him in his work.

nieto (son's/daughter's son).

novio ("fiancé"). The contacting of the opposite sex begins, for boys, at about the age of 15 years (see life-cycle). The initiative is generally taken by the boy. From fear of being turned down the boy often awaits some positive sign from the girl. A boy who has become known for "courting" several girls at the same time is called *muy enamorado* (very much in love).

Adolescencia: 18–marriage.

novio, desposado (bridegroom; see Life-cycle). The young men often choose their future wife for her beauty and personality, frequently, moreover, a poorer and less-educated girl so that the husband shall be able to play the dominant role in the marriage.

The girls often refuse to marry a young man who drinks, is known as a girl-chaser or is violent or lazy.

The civil marriage alone is contracted by young people who are poor.

After the marriage ceremony the bridal couple are admonished by parents and godparents before the household altar concerning their coming obligations. The man must always procure food, firewood and water for his wife, do necessary odd jobs in the home, abstain from excessive drinking or beating his wife.

Edad adulta: marriage–

marido (husband). It is the husband who is to dominate the family—at least officially. He keeps the family and represents it in the outside world.

In general the husband hands over his earnings to his wife, but sometimes keeps a part in order to strengthen his independence. If he uses the money for drinking he may be forced to hand it over on the initiative of the mother-in-law, the priest or the godfather at the marriage ceremony.

In order to maintain due respect the man is often forced to observe a certain distance to the family, which isolates him.

The great fear is that the wives shall become dominating and deprive the husband of his authority. This is often blamed on witchcraft, magic or poisoning.

The men are extremely jealous. They even renounce their friends to prevent contact with the wife. Only when she is pregnant does the man feel sure of her fidelity.

The man is the chief bread-winner of the family. He often opposes his wife's wage-earning work as this might be interpreted as an inability on his part to keep the family.

futuro padre (future father). A pregnant woman's husband must observe certain things, e.g. satisfy his hunger in order not to cause a miscarriage, or avoid coming home late in order not to render the childbirth more difficult.

padre (father). Officially the father is together with the mother responsible for the care and upbringing of the children, but the contact with the father is often made via the mother. The latter, like all the other female relatives, helps to maintain the respect for the father.

The father shows his love for the children by giving them money, or taking them to some fiesta, less by caressing or kissing.

The children show the father much respect, even fear, and in general behave well in his presence.

It is the children's duty to help the father when he is no longer able to work, but often the father has no confidence in the sons.

The father's death implies in the first place an economic loss, as he is the family's bread-winner.

padrastro (stepfather).

tio (paternal/maternal uncle). Paternal uncles and nephews extend mutual help to each other, but hostility may arise in matters of inheritance when a paternal uncle demands a part of the inheritance from his brother.

If the godfather of an orphan cannot meet his financial obligations, the *paternal* unlce replaces him.

yerno (son-in-law). Sons-in-law do not meet so often, especially if they live far from each other. Enmity frequently arises on account of inheritance.

padrino (godfather).
compadre (co-parent).
suegro (father-in-law).
viudo (widower).
abuelo (paternal/maternal grandfather).

THE FEMININE SEX-ROLES

Infancia: 0–2

criatura (see Life-cycle).

Niñez: 2–12 or 15

niña (see Life-cycle).

The girls' schooling is in a high degree dependent on how much they are forced to work at home, supervision by the mothers and an in principle negative attitude to their school education.

Adolescencia: 15–marriage

señorita. As from the girls' fifteenth birthday they are called *señoritas.* However, the improvement of their position is more apparent than real, inasmuch as their work and their responsibility are increased—becoming almost the same as those of an adult married woman. The care of the small brothers and sisters is entrusted almost entirely to them, but their authority is not complete; on the contrary, the smaller children take the mother's part in conflicts.

hija (daughter). The relation to the father varies from real fear to the position of favourite; especially does the latter apply to the eldest daughter, who when she is older often takes over the mother's tasks in relation to the father. The older she becomes, the more tasks does the daughter take over from the mother, but the mother constantly supervises her work and has the ultimate responsibility for its being well done.

hermana (sister). The eldest sister has the moral duty of looking after her younger brothers and sisters and she often shows them real tenderness.

However, conflicts arise when these duties hinder her own intellectual training.

The sisters must wait upon the brothers, who take this quite naturally: wash, iron, mend, cook food and serve them, etc. They must also help them in their love-affairs as intermediaries. A sister, on the other hand, never confides in her brother, this from fear of angering him.

Contact with the opposite sex is still surrounded with great secrecy as regards the girls, and a liaison that is brought to light causes them great unpleasantness, as a rule severe punishment and still stricter supervision.

It is often the girl who must encourage the boy to take the initiative to contact, but if she deliberately or unconsciously deceives him, the boy may take revenge.

Nowadays a girl has generally had several novios before she marries, even sometimes simultaneously, but this is not considered respectable, and such a girl is called *loca* (foolish girl).

novia (fiancée, bride). The fiancé's mother and godmother inform themselves concerning the girl's character, and if she is found to be lazy or disobedient at home, to have had many novios, to have gone out much by herself or has a weak constitution, they oppose the marriage.

The girl is admonished by her parents, in connection with her new life, to work much and obey her husband and parents-in-law, not to go out without her husband's permission and to avoid being jealous or a chatterbox. She is further admonished by her parents and godparents after the wedding to be diligent, serve the food punctually, keep the house clean, look after the children and help her husband.

A church wedding is considered to entail greater prestige. A merely civil wedding occurs only in lower social groups, in the case of women living alone, orphan girls without family-members who can insist on and back up a church wedding, pregnant girls and women with one or several illegitimate children.

Edad adulta

esposa (mujer) (wife). The ideal role of the wife as subordinate to the man and keeper of the home with responsibility for the family's welfare does not correspond entirely to the reality as regards submissiveness except outwardly and in official life. Her desire to attain greater freedom outside the home and to dispose over economic resources for her own use puts her in conflict with the traditional role and gives her a negative attitude to pregnancy and childbirth. Sexually she is completely subordinate to the man and in general has a lesser degree of *naturaleza* ascribed to her.

Even frigid women are generally preferred, as the man does not then need to be jealous.

Maltreatment of the wife is sanctioned if the wife has demonstrably been in the wrong, and if the beating is kept within reasonable bounds. The commonest accusations are infidelity, delayed meals, lack of cleanliness in the home, selling too much maize without permission, jealousy or inquisitiveness concerning the husband's doings.

futura madre (expectant mother). The expectant mother must observe a number of restrictions in order not to injure the child or complicate the delivery, e.g. not satisfy her longing for dainties, etc., in order not to risk a miscarriage, not to look at an eclipse of the moon lest the child be born with a harelip, not let a tortilla stick to the comal, lest the child get stuck at the delivery, etc.

madre (mother). The mother cares for and feeds the children and has the chief responsibility for their upbringing, at least in the home, both moral and religious. It is she who helps them, gives them advice, permission to do things, protection and tenderness.

The mother may show her tenderness openly by kissing and caressing the children, but also by adding to or diminishing her care, e.g. by giving them more food or devoting more time to their care. Consequently, the mother often has a favourite child, often the youngest son, but also sometimes the eldest.

The relation mother–child is more emotional than respectful, which is considered "natural". A mother who abandons her children is considered "abnormal" and is given the nickname *machorra*.

The mother's death implies in general an emotional loss.

When the eldest daughter reaches the age of 15 years the mother as a rule leaves almost the whole of the household work to her, thus getting greater freedom for her own interests, even if the greatest responsibility remains with her. (Cf. *nuera*—daughter-in-law).

madrasta (stepmother).

tia (paternal/maternal aunt).

nuera (daughter-in-law). The daughter-in-law must obey her mother-in-law as her own mother. The daughter-in-law often enters marriage with traditional notions that life with the mother-in-law will be slavery, which it often may be, though not so much as formerly. The oppositions between the generations in modern times militate more and more to the emancipation of the daughter-in-law. As soon as the young people are able to do so, they get a home of their own, but sometimes it is the old people who move.

cuñada (sister-in-law). The sisters-in-law visit and help each other, but there may also be hostility between them. In the majority of cases the wives follow their husbands' conduct.

madrina (godmother).

comadre (co-parent).

suegra (mother-in-law). The husband's mother regards her daughter-in-law as a grown-up daughter and treats her more or less like one. If the daughter-in-law is very young, not more than 12–13 years, it is the mother-in-law's duty to instruct her in the work in the home, and to keep watch on her fidelity to her husband. She must also assist the daughter-in-law at her confinement.

Great tension may arise in the relationship, and the mothers-in-law sometimes prefer poor and less pretentious daughters-in-law.

The man's mother-in-law, that is the wife's mother, often takes the man's part in domestic conflicts, as does also her father unless it has been observed that he really maltreats the daughter.

viuda (widow). Many widows do not dare to remarry on account of the children's negative reaction, and also on account of a feeling of modesty towards the grown-up children.

abuela (paternal/maternal grandmother).

As may be seen, life-cycles and sex-roles run rather parallel, something which is underlined by the author's deliberate adherence to the chronological order in his account.

Right from the birth of the individual the sex-difference is stressed socio-culturally with references to future functions and activities. Even if this emphasis is often only formal and symbolic, there does nevertheless remain the impression of a deeper import lying behind it, which influences the attitudes of the persons implicated.

The first more severely observed sex-difference in practice is that connected with toilet upbringing, which, even if it has a solid basis in experience, requires more of the girls than of the boys and this at a very tender age.

The first sex-differentiation on the part of the children themselves is seen in their games, which begin to imitate the activities of the adults.

The schooling involuntarily stresses the sex-difference inasmuch as the parents' traditional attitudes are applied differently to girls and boys. The former must work at home to help their mothers, which implies submission and isolation, while the boys have better chances for further education and, when they are needed as labour, get greater prestige earlier, as the fathers' work with which they are helping is valued higher.

Among the adults the sharpening of the starting-points of the socio-cultural sex-differences is further accentuated by the men's varying possibilities of activity, for instance in the political and administrative sector, while then women have, certainly, greater economic possibilities now than formerly, but only at a considerably riper age, often not until they have their traditional tasks as mothers and wives behind them. On the other hand, the women have difficulties in attaining to insights that make possible their activity in these sectors, but also in others, e.g. the ideological sector. Owing to their poorer attainments they must fall back upon what are frequently equally important and at least temporarily appreciated, but still less prestigious activities such as those of curandera, pharmaceutist, nurse, secretary, etc.

In other words, it seems as if the "field of influence" of the sex-roles has been extended beyond their actual application only as an expression for the individual's biological status, to include also secondarily acquired statuses and especially occupational status:

STATUS

```
male biol. s.   → sex-role ──────→ male role   ──────→ masc. roles
                                ↗                    ↗
                    age-status (→ roles)  other statuses (→ roles)
                                ↘                    ↘
female biol. s. → sex-role ──────→ female role ──────→ fem. roles
```

Instead of age-status or other statuses (e.g. occupational status) being expressed through respective *roles*, the influence from the sex-roles proper has allowed the construction of *male* roles and *female* roles, *masculine* roles and *feminine* roles.

Thus if it is to be possible to use the term "sex-role", it must be given the significance "expression for biological statuses" and consequently be used in the plural. "Sex-role" in the singular is only an expression for "man" or "woman". But since status has been defined as "the position of the individual in a social system", what system comes here into the question and what kind of "statuses" are these? If, further, "man" and "woman" are to be accepted as statuses, what form then will the roles have that are to give expression to them?

"La petite différence" has probably never been seriously called in question in the sex-role debate, but the disproportions in the socio-cultural sex-role difference cannot be explained away. Factors which have helped to confirm this, e.g. the Mexican *machismo* (cult of manliness), like those tending to eliminate this, e.g. the institution of godparenthood, which it has here not been possible to discuss, should be more closely studied in these connections.

REFERENCES

GOODENOUGH, WARD H. (1965) Rethinking "status" and "role". Toward a general model of the cultural organization of social relationships. In *The Relevance of Models for Social Anthropology*, A.S.A. Monographs 1, London.

LEWIS, OSCAR (1963) *Life in a Mexican Village. Tepoztlán Restudie*, Univ. of Illinois Press, Urbana.

HELLBOM, ANNA-BRITTA (1967) *La Participación Cultural de las Mujeres Indias y Mestizas el México Precortesiano y Postrevolucionario*, The Ethnographical Museum, Monograph Series, Publ. No. 10, Stockholm.

MADSEN, WILLIAM (1960) *The Virgin's Children. Life in an Aztec Village Today*, Univ. of Texas Press, Austin.

ZANTWIJK, R. VAN (1960) *Los Indígenas de Milpa Alta. Instituto Real de los Trópicos*, No. CXXXV, Sección de Antropologia Cultural y Fisica, No. 64, Amsterdam.

INVESTIGATION OF A VILLAGE IN
NORRBOTTEN, 1963-4

ANNA-MAJA NYLÉN

The Nordiska Museet, Stockholm

IN THE years 1963–4 an ethnological investigation of Svappavaara village, Kiruna municipality, was carried out by the Nordic Museum in collaboration with Norrbotten's Museum and the Central Office of National Antiquities. In 1965 a report on the results of the field-work was drawn up at the Nordic Museum. This exists in stencil form. The report consists in the main of a list of the material collected in the course of altogether $2\frac{1}{2}$ months' field-work in Svappavaara.

The collected material comprises mostly interviews with the informants, direct observations noted down and studies of photos, surveys and maps.

The chief aim of the investigation has been to record the present situation through this work—the present structure of the village in different respects—before the mining of ore which has been begun could have time to affect and change the village milieu.

The field-work has for the most part been performed by the recorders taking part from the Nordic Museum, and the investigation has been carried out with the help of grants from LKAB.

The initial situation for the investigation refers chiefly to data obtaining for the year 1964. However, the ore-mining in Svappavaara has been developed very rapidly and considerable changes may have taken place after that year.

Apart from an account of the scope and content of the material an account is given of the method for the investigation and of the principles applied in the preparation of the material for filing and of the persons taking part in the investigation.

By way of introduction there is a brief presentation of the newly started ore-mining in Leveäniemi, which chiefly occasioned this study; and in conclusion are given some views of the processing of the collected material.

The leaders of the investigation, Dr. Anna-Maja Nylén, the Nordic Museum, and fil.lic. Harald Hvarfner, Norrbotten's Museum, have not yet had time to penetrate and analyse the material and they therefore did not wish, when the symposium in the ethnology of the present was planned, to participate with a written contribution and lecture. However, as some of the lecturers intended to take part have defected, we have in response to a request drawn up the report as an example of the method of investigation together with some views regarding the processing of the material.

In view of these circumstances we hope that the participants in the symposium will accept with indulgence the submission of our contribution in this form. For our own part we find it valuable to have the opportunity of discussing the method of investigation, the recording and the documentation of data, and the views concerning and aims of the processing.

In the very first memorandum it is pointed out that the investigation has in the first place aimed at a recording of the milieu during a period of great and rapid change. In the course of the work we have also, as regards the external, visible aspects of the village, been able to note and photograph transformations of landscape and settlement that no other generation of inhabitants in Svappavaara has experienced. The resources which an enterprise like LKAB, with its assets, is able to put into a small village in the wilds are connected with the conditions on the world's market and with events of a political and economic nature with which the village inhabitants have nothing to do, but which will nevertheless shape their lives.

A similar situation existed when in the latter part of the seventeenth century, on the strength of the hopes vested in the copper deposits, Svappavaara became the object of the endeavours of the Momma brothers and their successors to carry on mining activities here. Despite the modest production which was maintained here for a time with much labour and small results, as compared with LKAB's achievements, it has in a remarkable way set its stamp upon the attitude of the village as this is reflected in hopes of a prosperity based on mining industry.

This phase in the development of the village may be studied in the archives of the Mines Authority and has in various connections been made the object for study and publication. Most recently the miner Albin Lindmark has published documents of the Mines Authority pertaining to the ore-mining in Svappavaara in the seventeenth and eighteenth centuries.

In celebration of the tercentenary of the discovery of the Svappavaara mine a work by Gustaf Tolonen was published. It deals with the earlier ore-mining in the village, but also with the occupations and life in other respects as these existed within living memory.

The present investigation, as mentioned above, was at first planned as an investigation intended to record the village milieu in process of change. In the course of the work there has been a certain modification of the collection of material. The comprehensive programme that was outlined in the first list of questions has been amended, in so far as after the first more summary collection of data over the whole field we decided to direct our activities in the sequel to certain definite regions and certain phenomena which on the basis of the notes and observations made we thought significant with reference to static and mobile components in the milieu.

What we here wish to record are the specific factors connected with Svappavaara's present situation. In point of time the material covers on the whole the conditions and trends of development from the outbreak of the Second World War until today, i.e. 1940 to 1965.

Since the mines in Kiruna and Malmberget have begun to be exploited industrial work has to a certain extent and in certain forms attracted labour also from Svappavaara. Thus the confrontation with industrial work existed before the location of ore-mining in the village. This, however, implied a much more intensive contact with industrial working life. It is considered that not only men but also women must be recruited as labour for the mine.

It is this confrontation of a Norrland village community with industry that we consider to possess an interest beyond that of a purely local-historic study. The situation is, of course, not unique. It applies and has applied for many Norrland villages. The meeting of industrialism with the agrarian mode of life as this manifested itself up to the Second World War, with extensive utilization of outlying lands for the collection of feed, of forests and water for hunting and fishing as a necessary complement, should be able to afford a sufficiently marked contrast to yield possibilities for theoretically important observations. On the other hand, this is a situation, as regards the adaptation to industrial working life, which characterizes the whole of our time all over the world.

It is a complete deluge of changes that have in a short time overtaken the village, with new people, new situations to be met collectively and individually, reorganizations of village plan and sites, settlement and dwelling and new valuations both material and ideal.

It has to a great extent proved possible to record the external changes, and we have been able to observe, describe and photograph adaptations of the external milieu to the new conditions. To observe how the traditional pattern for the form and function of the dwellings has been affected or retained has presented less difficulty than to observe the changes of the interior milieu. Here it has been necessary to knit a net of questions to seize reactions, adaptation to or rejection of the new valuations and attitudes entailed in the changed situation of the village. However, we have tried to record the ways in which the village has reacted collectively in the village meeting, in the church and political associations and in the family and the village inhabitants as individuals. To formulate questions that should cover significant conditions has been a difficult task with which we have not completely succeeded. The investigation will here probably need to be supplemented, even if adaptations of the external milieu to the new conditions are occasioned by and entail displacements in the inner milieu.

In an intensive investigation (punktundersökning') of this kind the spatial aspect is omitted. Also the chronological aspect is extremely restricted. The external situation is quite clear. All measures and developments of an economic and administrative nature are completely known. The documentation thus presents no problems and the processing can therefore be directed exclusively towards a study of the reactions of the individuals, the generations and the groups and the changes in the structure of the village community. The confrontation with an entirely new situation throws light upon the function of the social groups and the individual and of the customs, behaviour, the valuations and the material assets.

The specific conditions in the village, the religious sectarianism, the linguistic and demographic situation give an accentuation of the problem-complex that gives further interest to Svappavaara as a study-object.

We also find it of great methodological interest to define and study the functional aspect in order to ascertain what can be got out of a material collected entirely in the stratum of the present.

FRONTIER RESEARCH IN TORNEDALEN

HARALD HVARFNER and ASKO VILKUNA

Norrbottens' Museum, Luleå—Institute of Ethnology, University of Jyväskylä

NORDIC ethnologists have long been interested in different areas of distribution and contact zones. In spite of this, their researches have to a large extent had a national alignment. Through the regional differences which often exist in every country there have been objective grounds for a national delimitation. However, this has not been aimed at, but is rather a practical consequence of narrowing conditions in connection with the granting of subsidies.

In view of the general alignment of the research carried on by ethnologists it is a matter of course that a concentration of interest to regions with administrative boundaries of such a marked character as, for example, national frontiers may often give a sharper relief to the problems considered. The interest in questions around such boundaries here leads to inter-Nordic collaboration. This is what has happened in Tornedalen, the frontier zone between Finland and Sweden. As frontier investigations lead to inter-Nordic cooperation, so they lead also to inter-disciplinary collaboration. The problems around a frontier dividing a coherent settled area make themselves felt in all sectors of human community life and they can therefore not be investigated by a single discipline.

The floating frontiers have through the centuries been a constant source of irritation, the more so as the drawing of the frontiers has in the majority of cases been done over the heads of those most intimately concerned, viz. the frontier inhabitants.

One can—not least in Europe—find many labile frontier zones which would be excellently well adopted for inter-disciplinary, international research. That our choice fell upon Tornedalen is due not only to the circumstance that there is here a frontier which is close at hand as a research object and which separates two countries for which co-operation is possible; it is due above all to the fact that the frontier relations there may be described as stable, though this has not implied a complete elimination of the problems.

The Torne river was during the period of intensive settlement only a uniting factor. The lands belonging to the farmsteads might be situated on both sides of the river. As neighbours, the householders of the opposite bank were almost as close as those on one's own bank. Moreover, the Torne river, like many other big rivers in the provinces of Österbotten and Västerbotten, made of the settlers in its valley a social unit cherishing common values and a characteristic culture. Administratively it was always the aim to preserve the entities arising in the river valleys. The old boundary between the Uppsala and Åbo dioceses, for example, ran along the watershed between the Torne and Kemi rivers, which also separated Västerbotten from Österbotten. In the region for the old strand settlement the Swedish and Finnish languages meet between the Kalix and Torne rivers. This fact also supports the assumption of a homogeneous settlement in Tornedalen.

The drawing of the national frontier in the middle of the Torne river in the year 1809 was completely at odds with the basic character of the tract. Unlike many frontier rivers, however, the Torne river was able to a certain extent to keep its function as a uniting factor, which was in part thanks to the strong feeling of solidarity among the inhabitants of the tract. This feeling and the will to preserve the old district intact are now matter for great solicitude in the tract. This is testified to by the lively inter-activity of the associations working on both sides of the river and by the fact that it has been possible to eliminate the many sources of irritation caused by the frontier.

However, the frontier does undoubtedly hinder the spreading of certain culture elements. As regards legislation, political valuations and other governmental matters there are nowadays marked differences between the countries.

On the other hand, a frontier that cuts across a homogeneous area may be a culturally stimulating factor: two culture elements—one Swedish and one Finnish—can compete freely with each other under almost the same conditions. The contact is here often extended to embrace three countries: Norway is not far away. In the post-war period there have been many examples of what the contact between the three countries means in terms of stimulation in the northernmost parts of the three countries. There are today many realities behind the concept Nordkalotten.[1]

The national frontier in Tornedalen divides a uniform linguistic area. Parts of Swedish Norrbotten are now the only homogeneous Finnish-

---

[1] The Arctic area of the Nordic countries.

speaking area outside of Finland, and they thus constitute a very valuable area for studies in the Finnish language.

The ethnologist is interested in the question as to whether the language border can be parallel with the distribution border for any other culture element. In this connection the Kalix river-valley is an especially fruitful region, as the language border there divides a uniform culture region. For research it would also be important to find out what culture border the wasteland tract between the Kemi and Torne rivers constituted. In the Middle Ages, as we know, it formed both the diocesan and provincial border.

The function of the Torne river as a national frontier has right up to the present had a very prejudicial effect on the investigation of the river-valley. Investigators have hesitated to go over to the territory of the other country, and the time was not so ripe for personal cooperation between scientists before the last world war as it is today. It is on account of this and many other factors that the uncommonly interesting Tornedalen has not had the searchlight of research turned upon it. As there is in Torne-dalen a lively interest in acquiring a knowledge of the region as a culture area, it is a favourable conjuncture for the realization of a rather compre-hensive research. As Tornedalen unites Finland and Sweden, a Fenno-Swedish research group is a natural starting-point. The frontier problems obviously constitute a central task for research. There is probably not a better field for such a task in the whole of Europe.

In Tornedalen one can study the way in which culture elements cross and recross the frontier or are checked by this. One can investigate the appearances of culture borders and compare the administrative, linguis-tic and dialectal boundaries and the national frontier with one another and with the boundaries for the distribution areas for different culture forms and elements. As the tract is vast and thinly populated it offers sufficient dimensions also for the investigation of other frontier problems. An essential question is also how, in spite of the frontier, Tornedalen has been able to keep its unity intact. In this connection studies should be un-dertaken on the social significance of Laestadianism, common festivals, marriages over the frontier, visits to relatives and friends, information media, frontier trade, official co-operation and, in general, everything that may throw light on the peculiar cultural character of Tornedalen. It is also of importance to study the removals across the borders. In this connection changes in the structure of the population and variations be-tween the farmsteads and their number should be dealt with. In this way one approaches an investigation of the dynamics of the local culture;

and a couple of previously carried out village studies provide a good basis for this. At the same time one might take the time-limit as an object of study among the other boundaries.

Investigations on frontier questions are of great practical importance. From the international point of view it would doubtless be of value to draw attention to a characteristic frontier like the Torne river, which unites two nations, Finland and Sweden.

COLLABORATION IN THE STUDY OF FRONTIER PROBLEMS

For research in Tornedalen on the above lines a Swedish–Finnish research group with anchorage in Tornedalen, as well as in Finnish and Swedish universities, was formed at the beginning of the year 1964. In March 1964 the Culture Foundation for Sweden and Finland granted a sum for preparation and planning. Since 1965 the group has received grants according to a programme that has been approved by the Board of the Foundation. The group receives considerable practical support in Tornedalen, where the Tornedalen People's College has placed premises at disposal.

In the year 1964 we contacted researchers and institutions representing different branches of science. The response was in nearly all cases positive. It was decided that the period 1945–65 would be best suited for this research, that the work should be started in the year 1965 with field-studies and that there should be collaboration between above all the following disciplines: ethnogeography and social geography with community planning, economic geography, demography, sociology, sociology of religion, political science, ethnology and linguistics. As background for the studies general economic-geographic surveys and surveys on settlement, culture and church history and frontier policy would be needed. Selected macro- and micro-investigations were to be carried out in the field: on the one hand, for example, Tornedalen as a whole might be dealt with, and on the other hand comparisons might be made between a Swedish and a Finnish municipality or village, and trans-frontier files, "profiles", might be selected. These cross-sections were to be investigated in detail with the methods of different branches of science.

LANGUAGE AND FRONTIERS

As has been mentioned, Swedish Norrbotten contains the only Finnish-speaking region outside of Finland. As the schools there are Swedish-speaking and the official language is also Swedish, Finnish and Swedish have here different functions. The local Finnish dialect has been able to develop freely without the norms of the written language. In this way the dialect has acquired an archaic ring; but on the other hand, in the absence of Finnish neologisms it has been modernized with new Swedish words. The language border in the lower part of the research area has always been marked. It is therefore natural that an obviously Swedish influence on the colloquial Finnish of the Tornedalers cannot be observed to any considerable extent. But influence from their Finnish is, on the other hand, noticeable in their Swedish. The dialect form has been stable. Older people have still the same dialect form as prevailed there at the beginning of the century. The dialect on the Swedish bank of the Torne river is almost identical with that on the Finnish side of the frontier. The influence of Swedish is most noticeable only in some pecularities of sound, which are widespread and which thus developed early into a social norm (e.g. consonantal combinations at the beginning of a word and the sound f), and in the widely incorporated loan-words.

However, the national frontier has had the negative effect that although the population on the west bank of the river can speak Finnish, the people cannot write this language. There is thus a rather considerable bilingual reserve that might easily be used for a closer co-operation between Sweden and Finland.

The influence of the bilinguality on the Finnish can be most profitably studied in the westernmost and north-westernmost parts of the dialect area of Tornedalen. The use of Swedish and Lappish within a broad transitional zone has here for long been so common that it has had better possibilities of exercising an undisturbed influence on Finnish than in the river area. In these regions, moreover, one can find a great number of cases of bilinguality of different degrees in different age-groups, whereas the population in the Tornedalen region is in this respect necessarily rather one-sided.

The purely linguistic investigation is supplemented with certain philologico-sociological studies which deal with, *inter alia*, the distribution in different districts, ages, occupational groups and between the sexes.

In this connection are studied also certain philologico-pedagogic questions, e.g. the special difficulties in learning Swedish experienced by schoolchildren with a Finnish-speaking background. An analysis of the exercise-books of such schoolchildren may here yield valuable material.

From the language inquiry, which is under the direction of Docent Bengt Loman, Lund, emerge results of both linguistic and sociological interest, which also have a philologico-pedagogic value. The concrete descriptions of authentic, living colloquial and written language thus throw light upon the kind and degree of the intermingling of languages in bilingual persons and can also be taken as the basis for improved textbooks in the Swedish language for Finnish-speaking persons.

A tempting project is to study the language in a selection of schoolchildren now and then repeat this study after about 20 years with the same individuals. In this way one would get a clear idea of the direction language developments were taking. Such a study has not hitherto been made, nor has it been possible until now, when we have tape-band recorders with atis factory sound-quality.

COMMUNITY LIVING AND FRONTIERS

On the first planning trip in the northern Scandinavian area one of the participants was Professor Erik Allardt from Helsinki. He worked out a plan for sociological studies in Tornedalen, from which the following sis an excerpt.

The most urgent task from the sociological point of view is to chart *Tornedalen's social structure and value-milieu.* Sociological studies of social structure aim not only at giving an account of the distribution of the population according to different demographic criteria, but above all at an analysis of the social groups with which the population identifies itself and with which it feels solidarity. In analyses of social identification and basic ties of loyalty one can with advantage distinguish between a macro- and a micro-aspect. The macro-sociological analysis aims at studying the solidarity with national groups, organizations, political and religious movements, etc., whereas the micro-sociological analysis concentrates rather upon a study of intercourse with relatives and ties of friendship. One may here indicate three different problem-fields that seem central: (1) social structure and social identification in Tornedalen; (2) family structure, intercourse with relatives and conditions of friendship; and (3) orientations concerning values and attitudes to social changes.

Precisely the connection between different forms of orientation on values and attitude to technical improvements, economic and political modernization has engaged many sociologists in recent times. There are, of course, many different classifications of orientations on values and instruments for investigating these. It would be of great interest to try to ascertain whether central valuations (e.g. attitude to time; the past, which of the present and the future are considered the most important) are different in different parts of Tornedalen. Even without these ready made categories, indices and attitude-scales it would appear to be of interest to try to find out people's attitudes to traditions, technical changes, extension of the tasks of social welfare and so on in different milieus in Tornedalen. Are migration and actually realized technical improvements (in, for instance, agriculture) connected with the attitudes? Is the tendency to take initiative in the direction of modernization different in different groups and different on the two sides of the national frontier? Which groups constitute renewers, passive receivers or opponents of modernizations? Does the initiative to renewal come from national political or from local quarters? What role do officials play as renewers, passive observers or opponents?

FOLKLIFE AND BOUNDARIES

The ethnological working tasks in Tornedalen are various and comprehensive. It has therefore been necessary to impose considerable limitations in the planning of coordinated investigations. This limitation has been imposed after a careful planning of investigation-objects. These are representative for Tornedalen and therewith regionally typical, but at the same time they connect up with the general problem-complex which occupies the central position for the studies, i.e. the frontier questions.

As the ethnological studies take place in a transverse scientific context, it is important that they should be given such an alignment and delimitation that working material and results can be collocated with other research fields and supplement these. In the planning of ethnological fieldwork the other investigation plans that have been drawn up are therefore also taken into account.

The main stress in the ethnological investigations is intended to fall on the following:

1. *Systematic, locally delimited investigations* which are directed by Professor John Granlund, Stockholm. His concern is to find certain type-villages, e.g. Jänkisjärvi, where he carried out field-studies as early as the beginning of the 1930's and during the years 1945–8. In this way we also include the time-dimension. Jänkisjärvi and several villages in the vicinity are in a way nowadays not the most typical for Tornedalen's culture situation. It is therefore necessary to establish still a couple more research stations where the social and cultural picture presents another aspect.

2. *Theme and profile studies*. The main stress is here intended to fall on an investigation of traditional connection with the past and the spreading, absorption and adaptation of novations. The culture elements that

are chosen for detail study are together to enter in a common functional context which in a concentrated form is analysed in two or three locally delimited systematic studies.

The theme and profile studies link up with micro-studies running right across the valley which have been planned by representatives for other subject-fields in some selected places.

The ethnological investigations being carried out in Tornedalen are aimed especially at the following points.

To connect up with earlier ethnological studies of spreading phenomena in Tornedalen some traditional *working forms* are used which in today's situation have a breaking *or* stimulating effect in the general development of the frontier valley. In this context belong also questions relating to the use of time.

Further, *eating habits* and *diet* on either side of the borders give a material of value in this connection. As a main element bread has been taken up for a comparative study. This point is connected up with some questions pertaining to the physiology of nutrition.

The complex of object, custom and habit of milieu, which the dwelling may be said to be, is another important object, which is so complex that it leads over to systematic studies. Special attention is given to the change and design of dwelling in different social groups.

Groups studies may be chiefly concentrated on the following:
household groups;
working teams which may completely or in part coincide with the household groups but often extend further in the village, district and here sometimes over the national frontier—the study should be chiefly concentrated on their organization;
forms for intercourse outside of the working life, spare-time groups, especially their composition;
associations or societies with a certain definite aim, formal contra informal structure;
recruiting to centrally administered groups.

The group-studies are supplemented with *individual studies*. Particular attention is given to personal prestige in two to three chronological planes with point of departure from traditionally directed groups. The initiative inside and outside the groups is studied.

Tornedalen was to begin with a culturally homogeneous region. The investigation has so far been able to show how the homogeneity has been preserved, but also how new culture elements from today from national centres of dissemination have come to a halt at the frontier. One can follow the way in which a national frontier is constituted to form also a cultural boundary, to what degree and in what fields.

Owing to several factors with economically negative effect—often these are of a superficial nature—Tornedalen today appears as a developing region with different stages in different functions in Finland and Sweden. Where it is a matter of non-economic conditions—especially frontier questions—Tornedalen has in several respects entered a state of harmony which makes it from the international point of view one of the most important regions for frontier research, research on conflict and peace. It is our hope that a present-day oriented ethnology will be able to yield essential research results from the frontier region constituted by Tornedalen, perhaps results of fundamental importance.

REPORT OF AN INTER-NORDIC JOINT SCIENTIFIC RESEARCH PLAN: INSURANCE IN CONNECTION WITH THE CHILDREN'S BIRTH AND FIRST YEAR OF LIFE

LILY WEISER-AALL

Norwegian Ethnological Research, Oslo

ON 23–25 AUGUST 1965 Dansk Folkmindesamling (Danish Folklore Archives) held a symposium to discuss methods in connection with the collection of contemporary popular beliefs. The symposium was attended by thirteen representatives of Denmark, Finland, Norway and Sweden. Among the non-Danish representatives were only folklife and folklore researchers. From Denmark there were three sociologists and one psychologist. The point of departure for the symposium was provided by "informal discussions between Nordic folklore researchers experimenting with the collection of contemporary traditions" where it had been attempted to use statistical, sociological and psychological methods, and problems arising in this connection.

As a result of the proceedings the following subject was chosen: Insurance in connection with children's birth and first year of life. The investigation is to be transverse scientific and inter-Nordic. In Mr. Piö's report it is stated that "The following forms of investigation were suggested: (1) Study of tradition from the historical angle. (2) Investigations on the present (e.g. in the form of open questionnaires to midwives and nurses). Based upon this (3) representative investigation of a population. This was to be based upon an interest-determining investigation (pilot investigation). (4) Social anthropological method."

It was suggested that each country should publish its own results and finally a comparative study was to be made. The possibility of incorporating the investigation in the university tuition was mentioned.

As a preliminary basis for discussion I have drawn up a list of subjects which from the ethnological and Norwegian point of view correspond to the title chosen. As I thought that a new meeting would soon be held the only observation I appended to the draft was that it should be discussed jointly and the question of what demands may be made of informants and interviewers should be taken up.

The first section of the draft contains data required for the choosing of milieu. In connection with orientation concerning sexual questions and marriage planning a number of details are mentioned which are not to be incorporated in the questions but which should be noted if they come up, to help determine different degrees of orientation. This plan must be the same for the four countries and must be determined jointly.

The aim is to find the connection between the parental milieu and the actions that are to insure the child. By comparing data about the first points in the list of questions with actual attempts it was desired to find various relations, e.g. a resuscitation of the influence of the parents' own families, between the effect of theoretical notions of marriages mediated by different organizations. Further, a new valuation of the concept of the family may arise owing to a new situation. A relation will probably be found between definite degrees of orientation and later theoretical planning. Or one may find modes of action in spite of orientation and in spite of actual or imagined independence of the family. As well as all possible blends of courses of action. The advantage of the planned investigation combined with purely ethnological works is that psychological and sociological aspects will be assessed by specialists in these fields.

A further study of the subjects has led me to believe that one should attach greater importance to the form of wedding than originally indicated, viz. in connection with the question of the bridal dress in the cases of civil and church weddings respectively, the use of national costume, of old-fashioned bridal crown or urban dress, white dress with veil, use of a little bridal crown of silver that one can occasionally see in goldsmiths' windows in Oslo and other Norwegian towns according to Swedish pattern, the role of best man at the wedding and wedding party and so forth.

Information about wedding presents ought also to be fuller. The question of who gives presents should be defined: the members of the family, other relatives and intimate friends. Also of importance is information concerning the value of the gifts. One could in this connection ascertain whether older customs in the country districts with wedding gifts that were a real help for the new household are still being kept up. Material showing whether the customs connected with wedding presents in the country districts have changed is to be found in answers to questionnaires from Norwegian Ethnological Research. There is also material relating to older people in the country districts having a circle of friends, independently of kinship, neighbourhood and home-town, on the basis of common interests that have been cultivated in different associations. These also give wedding presents. It may probably be decided whether customs which give the impression of being urban customs are possibly customs from the countryside where they were taken over a long time ago by older generations.

The question-list contains some statistical data as an indication of what may be expected in general regarding popular belief in Norway in connection with births in hospitals. But there are a number of factors which enter here. There are situations of crisis and special states in human life which must be investigated and it is possible that popular belief will here play a role.

The subjects from popular belief that are mentioned in the list all occur in answers to Norwegian Ethnological Research from 1954 and later; among these have been taken only those of which it has been said that also the young people still believe and attach importance to. Among the last-mentioned subjects have been taken only those notions that I have also heard of in conversations in the towns and country districts. Whether it is on the whole possible to use questionnaires on these subjects that I have suggested I will discuss later.

QUESTIONS OF METHOD

Theoretically, there is no sharp distinction between research on popular belief and folklife and related sciences, so that the ethnologist can and must take up subjects that are also dealt with by other branches of science.

1. The old historical methods are usable if one puts the main stress upon present-day material. Historical background is necessary to be able to recognize and assess procedures, novations and actual changes. Without historical survey one cannot arrive at anything but a catalogue of present-day phenomena and this background is only one of the basic inquiries that an ethnological investigation demands. Where it is a matter of present-day material that one must collect in different ways a particularly careful source-criticism is needed.

2. Use of questionnaires. I think that in Norway one must proceed by experiment. There must be short, simple questionnaires for nurses, social workers, young mothers and fathers. But I think that one should attach greater importance to interviews and discussions on the basis of subject-lists which are drawn up for interviewers. These subject-lists should

be the same in the main points for all four countries. It will probably be necessary to hold orientating lectures in various organizations to find helpers. In talks with social workers aged about 30 years I got the impression that they do not at first understand that such an investigation is a scientific task. These are subjects that in their opinion they had no possibility of knowing anything about. After longer talks their interest was awakened, but in connection with the concept folklife research they thought of Norsk Folkemuseum (Norwegian Folklife Museum), the material must be old and anonymous, not "about us ourselves". They suggested, besides, introductory lectures in organizations that I precisely mentioned. As regards eventual questionnaires I noticed that young people have a dread of printed forms and identify these in their minds with the forms that must be filled up in maternity hygiene centres and at the doctor's.

A mixed use of interviews and questionnaires has, as we know, led to good results.

3. Verification of individual observations. For this work is needed, *inter alia*, an archive for all kinds of literature on subjects pertaining to the investigation, including articles in the daily and local press, publications of youth associations, radio talks and so on. In connection with this point I may mention that Dr. Olav Bö at the University of Oslo, Institute of Folklore, wants to give students of ethnology seminar exercises on the collection of such material for our subject, with discussions on the value of the material as training for later collecting and source-critical treatment of primary material.

4. Sociological methods. At preliminary inquiries at two sociological institutes in Oslo I was told that no researcher or student from there would in the immediate future be able to take part in the work, but interest in the plan was evident. At this stage of the plan I could only speak with persons with whom I was previously acquainted. There are other institutions that one may turn to when the plan has taken more solid shape with respect to the subjects and period to be investigated, and when one can say something definite about the financing. In Norway the greatest difficulty will be to find a sufficient number of workers to carry out the plan.

DRAFT FOR LIST OF SUBJECTS

Information about the informant:
    Man or woman.
    Year and place of birth.
    Religious denomination.

Place of domicile during adolescence.
Education and occupation.
Year and place of birth of father.
Father's religious denomination.
Father's place of domicile during adolescence.
Father's subsequent place of domicile.
Father's education and occupation.
Mother's year and place of birth.
Mother's religious denomination.
Mother's place of domicile during adolescence.
Mother's education and occupation.

Orientation on what the person concerned knew about sexual questions before marriage, planning of marriage, on inherited dispositions for serious diseases, rhesus-factor, kinship relation between marital partners. Eventual medical examination of both parties before the wedding. If it is a matter of knowledge or vague notions, where the person got these: discussions, courses in youth associations, clubs. Were these questions discussed in the family, what did the person learn about these in the higher school stages, from information among those of same age? Does person in question get information through books, newspapers, periodicals, weeklies, radio talks?

Desire for Children

From longing for children, on account of religious views or without the religious element in order to live a full human life, following pattern of own family. Does interviewee want to continue family-line, to increase social prestige? Do engaged couples take out a life-insurance before the wedding, men oftener than women?

Some men with dangerous occupations or who live in dangerous natural surroundings take out life-insurance oftener than women. Does interviewee consider it important for wedding to take place on a "favourable" day? Are there traditions, or is advice sought from fortune-tellers, eventually on grounds of horoscope for the engaged couple? (In Oslo especially Saturdays are preferred in case of civil wedding. One of the reasons is that then the ceremony takes place at the Town Hall in a handsome room, on other days at the courthouse, a less festive place.)

Wedding

Family gathering, who is invited. Company and church wedding out of consideration for the family. Civil wedding with family gathering. Civil and church wedding.

Who gives and what do the presents consists of? What is the opinion about wedding presents consisting of outfit for a future child?

Pregnancy

If no child comes within a reasonable time will any steps be taken?, gynaecological examination, eventual operation, insemination. Are there other possibilities, e.g. household remedies, and of what do these consist? Who gives such remedies, older female relatives or acquaintances, fortune-tellers, is prayer resorted to?

Many do not get married until a child is expected. Is marriage entered into to ensure mother and child, from consideration for family, reasons of prestige?

The attitude of the mother to an unwanted child often becomes positive in advanced stages of pregnancy. Especially in the first two months states of depression in the pregnant woman are common, is this known?

Is pregnancy, apart from normal discomfort, a good time for the woman, the feeling of being in harmony with Nature?

Is the man aware of the pregnant woman's mental and physical discomforts and troubles, does he show consideration on this account?

Does the pregnant woman read books on pregnancy, older books that may be available or the newest she can get?

Is the questionee afraid of congenital defects, mother more than father?

Does the pregnant woman go regularly to the maternity control centre or does she get advice from her doctor, does she follow the advice?

Does she use medicines on her own, household remedies?

Who gives household remedies, relatives, female fortune-tellers?

Among the advice is what a pregnant woman should eat and what she may not eat.

To avoid having children with congenital defects, the pregnant woman must eat what she feels like, small portions where it is a matter of harmful food, but never suppress desires.

Many still believe that the child may be affected by what the pregnant woman sees. Does this hold for the whole pregnancy or only certain periods?

The first two months, the time when the fetus "gets life", i.e. when the mother feels its first movements, or the last months. How does the pregnant woman avoid seeing what may affect the child adversely: shall she not see ugly people, animals, things, pictures, cripples, injured persons, corpses, conflagrations? It is particularly dangerous when the pregnant woman smiles at or makes fun of cripples, will the fetus then get the same defects the mother has smiled at?

May she not see a living or dead hare, will the child get a harelip?

In Norway sportsmen cut off the muzzle of a killed hare or wrap it with paper. In Oslo one practically never sees a hare with uncovered head in the display window of poulterers. In 1965 it was confirmed that this is to protect pregnant women from seeing the hare's muzzle.

May she not see snakes? The consequence for the fetus: snake's eye (it is no longer known what snake's eye is, often nystagmus, also black eyes), snake's skin, congenital scaly skin, congenital cleft tongue? Often the consequence of the mother's seeing unsuitable persons or objects is that the child gets birthmarks of the same form as what the mother has seen.

The pregnant woman must avoid touching her body, especially her face, when she gets a fright, as the child will get a birthmark in the same place that she touches.

Can she therefore place the birthmark, when a misfortune occurs, in a less embarrassing place in the child by immediately clapping her hand to her thigh or buttocks?

Must she see beautiful things to get beautiful children? Must she be gay to get gay children?

Is it believed that excitement, anger and sorrow result in nervous and mentally feeble children?

Must the pregnant woman avoid hard work, or is heavy work not harmful, but results in an easy birth?

May the pregnant woman not let herself be photographed (why)? Do the parents want a boy as first child, the fathers more than the mothers?

Is a child of the opposite sex desired for the next birth? Is the pregnant woman afraid of the confinement, is the man afraid?

If no fear is felt, is this due to a confidence in medical help that approaches superstition?

The Birth

At the maternity clinic. In Norway 97 per cent of all children are born at a clinic; 99·9 per cent in Oslo and Bergen, 99 per cent in several count-ies, 90·3 per cent in Troms, 92·3 per cent in parishes and fjords, 93·6 per cent in Nordland.

At the clinic there is no reason to observe old customs at the birth and first child care, but one can observe a belief in omens in connection with the child's birth.

Time for birth. Odd or even hours, midnight, early morning, before noon, after noon, at dusk. The interpretation of whether the birth-hour bodes well or ill often varies in one and the same district. The same applies for the majority of the following omens. This difference may be due to old tradition.

Has the weather, especially the wind, at the birth-hour any significance for the fate of the child?

Day of birth. Is a Sunday-holiday child (Christmas, Easter, etc.) generally considered a lucky child?

What does the expression lucky child imply? Is it a vague mode of speech or is something definite intended, e.g. that a lucky child is successful in all he undertakes, protection against illness, sudden death, hornet sting, snake bite, etc.?

There are rhymes about the significance of days of the week for children, e.g.: "Monday's child is fair of skin, Tuesday's child gets an amiable disposition, Wednesday's child must suffer much, Thursday's child will travel far, Friday's child has luck in love, Saturday's child must sigh with sorrow." Otherwise Friday's child, more rarely Thursday's child, is often considered unsuccessful.

Month of birth. Birth under a certain constellation in the zodiac has significance for the child's character, fate and duration of life. Formerly one could read of this in almanacs, where do people now get this information (weeklies, radio talks)? What is the signification of a child being born at new moon? What significance have the seasons of the year?

Is it considered fortunate when the child is born (1) with caul, (2) in the whole fetal bag?

Uncommon marks. What does it signify for the child to be born with eyebrows growing together, with teeth, with curls, with whirls in the hair? (All these marks may be of good or ill omen.) Are small birthmarks in the face considered lucky or beauty spots? Ought every child to have a birthmark? Can birthmarks in different places on the body have a different signification in accordance with the place on the body where they are located?

First-born. Has the first-born particularly good abilities, also "supernatural" abilities, e.g. ability to extinguish conflagrations, or is he or she predestined to be a fortune-teller?

Twins. Is it believed that twins are a misfortune, as they are weaker in physical and mental respects than other children? Is it believed that when a twin dies, the other becomes a fool (feeble-minded)?

Are congenital defects considered to be God's punishment for the mother's, parent's or forefathers' sins?

Is a tree or other plant planted at (the first) child's birth or baptism, and is the flourishing of the plant associated with the child's welfare?

Is there belief in a connection between a child and a domestic animal born at the same time?

Birth in the home. What is the reason for a woman's giving birth at home? If there is knowledge of remedies for a difficult birth are these nevertheless used when the midwife does not come in time, or when she, too, is at a loss?

What kind of remedy (shaking, lifting and the like), what kind of homemade medicines are available to aid delivery? Can the confinement be hastened and eased by the laying on of hands, what must be said at the same time?

Are joint prayers resorted to, in order to help the delivery, is money promised to the church, alms to the poor?

Do the questionees know the following remedies for hastening and easing the birth: the confined woman must confess her sins, especially sexual offences, to those present?

How many persons are present at a birth in the home? Only adult women, do men (except the father of the child) and children leave the house or the room?

What kind of remedies and medicines are available for hastening the casting of the *after-birth?*

Can one remove disfiguring birthmarks on the newborn by wiping them with the child's after-birth?

Are parts of the after-birth and the caul hidden away, or what is done with them?

Cutting the umbilical cord without the help of a midwife. Is the cord cut at once or only after the casting of the after-birth? Is the cord doubled over in two places and then cut between the two tied off parts?

Is the cord tied off and cut outside the tying off?

What is the ligaturing done with: woollen thread (there are popular sayings about this), other thread that is available, horse-hair?

Is the navel-stump hidden away after it is has dried and fallen off? Is the dried navel-stump used as medicine?

Is something put on the navel wound, e.g. a 5-öre piece or a raisin, so that the navel shall be beautiful and to avoid inflammation.

First washing or bath-water. Is anything put in the first washing water, e.g. salt, a fiery red bit of wood, inherited silver? Is care taken not to hang out baby clothes to dry after sunset? Is a psalter, page from a psalter or Bible, scissors, coin, inherited silver, a piece of bread put in the child's first bed until baptism? When the child is born in a clinic these old customs may be observed after the child is brought home. Does this happen when an older relative, the grandmother, lives together with the young couple?

Witch's milk. The breasts of newborn boys and girls sometimes swell up and contain a milk-like liquid. What is it believed this is due to? Is a name for the liquid known? Is it believed that the liquid must be pressed out, and is this done?

Suckling. When the child is born at home. Fore-milk (colostrum) is often thought to be dangerous for the child, what is it given instead, e.g. sugared water, tea, porridge, or is it suckled by another woman?

What time must elapse before the mother is to suckle the child herself?

Are means known for increasing the milk production, e.g. drink much water, milk, tea, eat fish soup and fish?

Is the only means that can help, viz. for the breast to be sucked quite empty, known? What is done to achieve this if the child does not do it? Is a hand-pump used to empty the breast?

Is the mother's milk examined at the maternity control centre and is the feeding of the child ordered in accordance with the directives given there?

Is the questionee in the habit of suckling her children or does she resort to artificial feeding at once (bottle-child)?

Does a boy need more mother's milk than a girl? Are boys breast-fed for a longer time than girls? For how long is the breast generally given?

What kind of old remedies are used at the weaning?

How are times arranged for the suckling, do the mothers, for example, change the time-scheme from the clinic on account of the rhythm of the home?

When the child screams between meals is recourse had to a lolly-pop, or old-fashioned string, a linen cloth with soaked ship's biscuit and sugar, porridge, bread or other (chewed) food?

Are tablets given to get the child to sleep?

Visits to the feeding mother. Is the feeding mother visited at the clinic and at home, and is it chiefly women that come? Does she get any particular kind of food (e.g. sponge-cake) from the visitors and the child a little gift (money)?

If someone happens by chance to come to a house where there is a new-born child should the person in question give any money to the child?

Is a man's hat or cap taken from him and must he pay a money forfeit to the child to get his hat back?

Is there anyone who believes that favourable omens at the hour of birth, etc., or the caul is sufficient insurance for the child's fortune?

Economic insurance. Is it common to give a bank-book to the newborn? Do boys get a larger sum than girls?

In Oslo the Oslo Savings Bank gives every newborn child a gift-card for a bank-book with 10 kroner. One must oneself fetch the bank-book, is anything deposited in this bank-book also later? Do other banks in other towns give such a gift-card to every new-born child?

Is a life-insurance for the child taken out? Does the father or mother take out a life-insurance policy at the child's birth, if they have not done so before?

Does the newborn child get other gifts than money and from whom? In the country districts gifts at birth were not a general custom, with the exception of well-to-do farmers who gave to both boys and girls a piece of land, a wood, a domestic animal, especially if the latter was born at the same time as the child; is this the custom today?

Does the mother get a gift from her husband on the occasion of the first birth or at every birth?

Children born out of wedlock: what does the mother do to insure the child's future?

Are unmarried mothers oriented concerning the benefits given by the authorities to illegitimate children? This latter seems not always to be the case; many also allow themselves to be frightened by forms that must be filled up and give up half-way. What do the authorities do for the instruction of unmarried mothers; how do the maternity control centres in the country districts function?

Is it still believed that it is possible to hasten and ease the delivery by stating the name of the child's father?

Baptism. In Norway 98 per cent of all newborn children are baptized, 96 per cent in the established church and 2 per cent in other Christian denominations.

Is the child baptized for religious reasons, to assure it a status, from consideration for the family, for accepted practice and tradition?

Is it believed that the child is exposed to various dangers (what kind) before the baptism and that baptism is the best protection?

Is the mother afraid of the child's dying without being baptized, does she therefore want to get it baptized as soon as possible and resort to emergency baptism without priest?

Who performs emergency baptisms (preferably men)?

Baptism in the home occurs in Norway as far as is known only as emergency baptism, and the child is subsequently baptized in the church at a suitable date.

For how long do people otherwise wait with baptism? What fate awaits a child that dies without being baptized? Must an unbaptized child not be mentioned by the name it is to get at baptism?

Choice of name. Is the first-born to be named after the father's parents, the next after the mother's parents?

Are children to be named after living or dead relatives? It is often related that the mother dreams that a deceased relative requests that the child shall be named after him or her. Is such a request complied with? How otherwise is the name chosen? Is the child named after sport stars and film stars, other famous persons, members of the royal family?

Does the namer ascribe to the name such significance that the child is expected to become like the namesake? Is this last view also held in connection with the choice of godparents?

What is today expected of the godparents, e.g. baptismal gift, gifts on later red-letter days in the child's life, e.g. confirmation?

When does the obligation of the godparents to give presents to the godchild cease?

Can a person refuse to be godparent?

Is financial support expected over and above what has been mentioned, advice in important decisions from the godparents?

How do the godparents fulfil their promise to see to the Christian upbringing of the godchild?

Who is not requested to be a godparent, e.g. a pregnant woman (why)?

Baptism. What kind of christening clothes are used, white dress and bonnet? Are christening clothes of other colours used? Are there old christening clothes that are used? Are christening clothes lent?

Is the caul concealed in the christening clothes so that it is baptized together with the child?

Who carries the child during the ceremony of baptism?

Does it signify anything if the child screams, sneezes or prattles during the ceremony?

What is the consequence if some word is omitted in the form for baptism, when the priest stammers, clears his throat or coughs?

Is the child received at a special meeting in the home after the baptism, is it at once laid on a table, the floor?

Must the child sleep in its christening clothes (why)?

Is a child-christening party performed in the home or in a restaurant with family gathering? Who is invited?

Is the entertainment, the meal more lavish when the child is a boy, the first-born child, than when it is a girl or a subsequent child?

If the child is not baptized, is the naming marked with a gift or an entertainment?

Child care in the home. Do expecting mothers go through a course in child care, do they read books on the subject, are they helped by relatives?

Does it happen that children are swaddled, also the arms?

If the mother goes to the maternity control centre, does she follow the instructions given?

Is it thought that illness and indisposition that are not considered dangerous are "part and parcel" of infancy and need neither medical inspection nor treatment? Are household remedies used in such cases, and what kind? Are tablets given without consulting medical opinion?

Is it known that mortality among infants is highest in the first year, higher for the first-born than for subsequent children, higher for boys than girls?

Is medical attention sought oftener for the first-born, for boys than girls and later children?

Is there any household remedy to ease the eruption of the teeth, against cramps connected with the eruption of the teeth; is the child given anything to chew on, is anything, e.g. peony-seed, hung round the child's neck, are home-prepared medicines, e.g. decoction of the child's navel stump, dried after-birth used?

Does the person who discovers the child's first tooth get a little gift, or must the person in question give the child something? Does the child otherwise get a gift in connection with the first tooth, and who gives the "tooth"-gift?

ETHNOLOGY OF THE PRESENT—
THEORETICAL AND PRACTICAL
POSSIBILITIES

KNUT KOLSRUD

Institute of Ethnology, University of Oslo

I PRESUME that the question of the ethnology of today is something other than the use of traditional material for the reconstruction of earlier ways of life.

I see the place of contemporary studies in folklife research or ethnology in the first place as a question of the theoretical connection with historical ethnology. Is there, in other words, anything fundamentally new that is added and distinguishes this field from the traditional ethnological studies? If this is the case I should think it rather dubious to tackle problems which may be better studied in well-established contemporary disciplines. If, on the other hand, this is not the case, one may ask oneself what identification there may be between historical and contemporary ethnological studies. And on this basis one may ask oneself what is the nature of the tasks that naturally fall under ethnological analysis in our time.

If, now, as is reasonable, one proceeds on the assumption that ethnology is an independent science, this means that its theory, its aims, concepts and methods determine the nature of the problems and the choice of the material. It gives priority to its most important tasks from its own inherent conditions and not from presentations of problems in other disciplines. From this point of view ethnology carries on, as do also, of course, all other disciplines, "buttonology" (*knappologi*)[1]. Important questions in ethnology may be as meaningless for neighbour-sciences as central problems in these may be meaningless for the ethnologist. The ways of storing fishing tackle may be of essential importance for an understanding of its place in the folk-culture. The same has hardly any particular interest for political or economic history, whereas, on the other hand, the use of the tackle in Lofoten waters may have a certain importance.

Thus when Nordic ethnology works with our historical folk-culture it

---

[1] Satirical coinage by August Strindberg against typological archaeology (... buttons with and without holes ...).

is obviously not restricted by anything but that which may reside in the initial concept, in the subject and in the methods and the materials that may be used. The tasks will therefore be to ascertain whether the concept folklife or folk-culture is something historically defined, something that no longer exists, or whether there resides in this concept something which implies identity between past and present.

I shall not here attempt a documented presentation of the shifting content of the concept folk-culture. I will try rather to point to a couple of general features in ethnological research which will, I think, show that it may be theoretically justified to use the term folklife of forms of life in today's community. Problems centering around these forms of life will be *knappologiske* and perhaps unsystematic auxiliary questions in the periphery, so to speak, of the central theoretical tasks of other disciplines. However, they may occupy a central enough position for ethnological studies which are connected with historical ethnology.

Folk-culture is probably understood by the majority of ethnologists as the life-forms of regular character which characterize the anonymous historical personality when he appears as one of the many in the historical social groups. This mass concept in itself implies that he does not appear as creative in the sense in which named historical personalities are who "make history". On the contrary, he is a practiser of cultural norms when he carries on his occupation, builds his house or lives in it with his family. When one reconstructs these life forms ethnologically on the basis of traditional or historical material it is these regularities that constitute the folk-culture.[2]

Eilert Sundt strongly emphasized that the study of peasant culture must take "the general" as a basis and not bother about the deviating features. His concept of the peasantry and its life-form is admittedly a construction, a statistical mass: one does not have a scientific result until one collects the many according to their resemblances under one roof and the separated individual disappears. When such descriptive generalizations are attained one may go on to put these generalizations of the material

---

[2] A word of argument is here possibly necessary to clarify this position in view of Mr. Blehr's previous paper. The interpretation which he makes of the concept of culture and specifically folk culture in the Scandinavian folk life studies is a distortion of the relationship between observed data and their regularities in the form of verbal or numerical generalizations in the analysis. It is evident that the descriptive generalization presented as "culture" can not be identical with the totality of behaviour, whether observed directly or indirectly in the historical dimension or in the "material culture". To understand such generalizations as reification of culture and the individual as reduced to an automaton in behavior is a confusion of abstraction.

in relation with one another to find "connections" in the proper sense in the folklife.[3]

Sundt has only thought in a system which presupposes a functional connection between the elements in the system. The system at any level in the historical dimension is axiomatically constructed so as to imply interrelations.. A "historical" explanation of a historical phenomenon consists, therefore, in using contemporary factors in the past to explain the existence and in part form of the phenomenon. It has even been asserted that the basic function of a phenomenon is identical with its origin. In all cases historical explanations of change must, precisely, find contemporary factors, if the explanation is to be systematic and not restricted to the statement that a_2 exists because a_1 has existed. Thus if by ethnology of the present one understands the study of synchronous connections between elements or aspects, there is no theoretical difference between historical ethnology and ethnology of the present.

The basis for such a view of modes of explanation that abolish the difference between today and yesterday is that the popular cultural forms are seen from a somewhat different angle than that which is perhaps more widespread in the culture science. In a way, the characteristic ethnological explanation is "multi-disciplinary", i.e. the system one works with is abstracted from "reality" in a slightly different way than many other fields of study.

The object for the study of art, for instance, is only the culture manifestations which satisfy certain aesthetic criteria of value, or in other words the tradition in one aspect of the life-form in the community. The study of boats may be a part of the history of navigation, and the boat may be analysed as a technological sequence in an evolution and be therewith regarded as an abstraction from the total life-form in which the boat is a link. The boat does not become an ethnological subject until as a part of this life-form it is related to other aspects of it, e.g. the crew, the fishing tackle, settlement, occupation on land, etc. Similarly, ethnological art, I believe, is something other than the art-historian's subject.

Such "multi-disciplinary" analysis of entities does not of course mean that everything is to be explained by everything, but it does imply an analytic attitude that leads one on to problem-complexes of an in part different

---

[3] Again for the sake of argument: Material artifacts and "customs" may or may not be treated in the analysis as culture elements. The content of "element" in cultural studies is obviously dependent on the kind of problem under investigation, the type of material available, the level of abstraction, and the concepts used in the analytical process.

kind than in the special culture disciplines. Thus the curriculum in the study of folklife research consists of apparently extremely disparate subjects, from agriculture to art and social groups which, taken separately, are parts of other sciences. It must be the connection between these aspects that gives ethnology an independent task and defines its special methodology.

I presume that it is from such a viewpoint one must evaluate the possibility of ethnological research on the present. A large number of disciplines have aspects of the present as object of research. But ethnology can in the face of our complicated contemporary scene not pretend to any "multi-disciplinary" synthesis or enter into the different technical theories and techniques in our contemporary sciences. How, then, is it to become possible to do anything of today? And, furthermore, do it with the methodical attitude which contains ethnology's tools for problems in the past and eventually the present, in other words, while retaining the identity as a discipline with which I started?

I must then revert to the mass concept as essential for an understanding of folk-culture. By mass is meant not only a large number of individuals, but also the collective in which the individual chiefly lives. This anonymous historical personality is the bearer of the cultural regularities that ethnology reconstructs and finds connections between. He is a "user" of cultural norms which he has adopted from others in the little community in which he spends his life. Historically, these individuals have small possibilities of choice, partly on account of the standardizing pressure of the group, partly owing to the relatively few impulses from without. One may therefore say that practically speaking the ethnologist works with the "traditional" culture both in time and space.

But a presentation of the traditional element in the life-forms is still a secondary description of the thing itself and has not necessarily the generally valid theoretical character that would enable it to define the subject-field of a science. The primary reality is the fact of the anonymous historical personality continuing to live among us as a user of the community's cultural norms in the little group to which he belongs, and who in the enumeration gives the statistical tendency. In certain such groups he has little or no freedom of choice, like the crane operator when he unloads a ship in port or as chief accountant in an enterprise. Technical and administrative knowledge gives him the norms. It must be obvious that ethnological science has no possibility of analysing such preconditions for his work, or the economic considerations of the leaders or the constellations of power behind the shaping of working life. This is central control which must be taken as the antecedence condition for the system of life-forms to which persons in the mass must conform. The problems concerning the origin and central integration of such norms thus falls outside the scope of ethnology of the present.

But both crane operator and chief accountant once chose their occupations, and they live, moreover, in a world of ostensible choice between possibilities, for instance between friends and within the family. They have spare time, and they dispose over incomes in accordance with which they shape their own and their families' ways of life. They are, in other words, users of both traditional and at their choice new cultural norms which in the present have little by little become far more numerous than in former times. What do they use of the cultural possibilities available today, what in the aggregate constitutes their way of life, and why do they do this? The folk-culture of our time may be understood as the regularities in the life-form of such groups in all fields in which the individual combines traditional patterns with what he chooses from the contemporary scene.[4]

Without any theoretical, methodical or material break with historical ethnology I think I may conclude that ethnology of the present may best be developed as a workaday consumption-study of objects, norms and behaviour in the very widest sense in those aspects of the life of the small groups which are not incorporated in central systems of institutions. It retain its "multi-disciplinary" character, seen from the standpoint of other sciences, in the attempt to see a whole which does not include everything in the community and therewith be of use as an independent science.

The family, for instance, is therewith not only a social structure of interest for sociologists, but also a broader system of objects, of consumption and the giving of priority to income, to customs and usages, to conceptions of value, and aims in life. This mode of life, in so far as it can be revealed as regular, must have inner connections between its aspects and elements about which ethnology ought to have possibilities of theorizing. And these connections or structures of objects, roles and conceptions in the little community undoubtedly lead one into general culture-processes, e.g. mechanisms of distribution, as in historical ethnology.

---

[4] Axiomatically extreme is then the view that cultural forms can generally be understood from rational choices as they are acted out in regularities in a synchronic and/or diachronic dimension. The generation of forms has an equivocal meaning, and the lack of relevant material for analyzing rationality in the historical dimension may easily lead to circular reasoning about action-values-action. Mr. Blehr's own interpretation of Lønborg's article is a beautiful example of this fallacy.

The methods one would use purely practically for the collection of material I do not consider necessary to discuss in principle, since it is not these practical aspects of the matter that define a science. They may be borrowed from other disciplines to the extent to which this may be practically useful for the problem-complexes emerging from the theoretical basic attitude. And this discipline is based upon an identity between historical ethnology and ethnology of the present and must justify ethnology in not being a discipline delimited in time or by a cultural type.

I find it necessary, however, to discuss another aspect of the problem of ethnology of the present. The purely theoretical possibilities for our science to abolish the difference between historical and contemporary problem-complexes are one thing. Quite another thing is the circumstance that the sciences have a social function, tasks which are to be solved on the basis of social values. An academic study that is to give a scientific foundation for later work is not merely theoretically developed. It must take the labour market into consideration.

An academic activity can thus not be carried on in a theoretical vacuum. It must have a function in the community in order to be viable at all. It must, in other words, be associated with a socially important field of activity that has posts to offer. The field of work of these posts will in a high degree stamp and modify the shaping of the subject, for example in so far as the practical tasks will give priority to the admitted problems that must be solved, e.g. the dating of a house or the reconstruction of a temporally correct inventory of the objects in the house.

But this interaction between theory and practice leads not only to a conventional giving of the priority to certain tasks which may give the impression of constituting the central subjects in the discipline. It may also give impulses towards fresh thinking of a more fundamental nature in relevant sciences. The functional orientation has not only its origin in theoretical considerations or impulses from other sciences or in the problems of explanation with which one is confronted in the field-work among so-called "history-less" culture. It is also a matter of purely practically enticing people to museums to create an interest in the community which is necessary in order to get an economic basis for the carrying on of such institutions and so afford conditions for the scientific activity of the discipline. An example is the transition of several museums from exhibitions a couple of generations ago in endless typological series of native objects to attempts to compose milieu pictures of objects in connection with one another and together with human beings in order to appear more living and attractive to the public.

These endeavours raised a number of problems, especially in connection with the problem of creating milieu pictures that were representative for the division in culture regions. This led to theoretical speculations concerning the elements, complexes, aspects and geographical and historical processes of the culture. Concepts like diffusion and convergence, culture-areas and -centres, boundaries and composition have, as far as I understand, acquired more precise import and become subject for more topical debate from this point of departure.

The scientific independence and internal connections of culture phenomena have, as we know, been strongly accentuated and deepened in discussions sprung from the social situation of ths area of knowledge. It is thus lines from the practical tasks to the more fundamental discussion of concepts that take one to the divisions of the reality of which a discipline consists, which equip us with the forms of thought with which we tackle a "whole".

In the study of folk-culture this connection seems to be rather clear between applied and academic ethnology. I should like to quote Professor Sigfrid Svensson, who expresses the matter thus:

> The subject of folklife research is the popular culture. As popular is understood here the culture which through the way it is bound to tradition and its group or local stamp differs from the international culture ("upper-class culture", "mobile culture", "high culture") which is constantly in the throes of rapid changes. In connection with this the "most centrally emphasized part of its material" lies "in a stock of objects preserved in the field and in the *museums*... or in *folk-traditions* noted down or surviving in the present".

This is a well-known and concentrated characterization of the orientation of Nordic ethnology. It delimits the discipline to the locality bound culture-variants and to the little variable elements that are preserved in museums, archives or the people's memory or are to be found as relics in our time, in other words: are in process of disappearing.

The fact that the material for ethnology is in process of disappearing or is "preserved" in museums and archives has given grounds for a technical definition which is based upon the material rather than on a theoretical culture definition. It leads one on to problems and methods which probably give occasion for structure analysis in the past, but prevents one from seeing relics and traditions as functional in relation to new elements. Thus when these have finally disappeared one will be prevented from applying the more controlled mode of investigation that the contemporary gives grounds for. Forms of thought and acknowledgements can thus be limited in a way that is not happy for ethnology as an independent science.

Now, however, the great majority of scientific posts in the discipline are precisely connected to "the institutions for preservation", especially the museums. And the question then becomes: does this labour market afford any real possibilities for synchronous contemporary studies of the kind that can be theoretically justified? I do not, unfortunately, believe it is possible for the museums to change character fundamentally, and this will therefore affect the way of posing the problems.

The museums as archives for our material culture have not been built to preserve this in its entirety for scientific acknowledgement, but to satisfy certain basic community values. This may be illustrated by the growth of the museums in Norway, which I presume represents something of the orientation of values and perhaps also the giving of priority that reside in the community.

I shall not dwell on the phase in which more or less systematic collections originate from a diffuse desire to know about natural historical and cultural rarities and curiosities. I shall occupy myself with the significance of the sequence in time that the founding of several types of museum seems to imply. It is a matter of the more systematic public interests for culture-historically valuable collections.

The interests which are earliest expressed in Norway and which thus build upon the generosity of the public as the foundation for the institution are the *antiquarian* interests. It is typical that the archaeological collections in Trondheim, Oslo and Bergen are the country's oldest museums. And the natural-historical collections in Stavanger and Tromsö which now contain archaeological sections were added in the second half of the century.

The interests which next gave results in the form of independent public institutions were the *aesthetic* interests. Our National Gallery and the Art Gallery in Bergen and the Art Society in Trondheim were founded in the first half of last century. And in the second half the museums of art industry in Oslo, Bergen and Trondheim were founded.

Also *exotic* interests asserted themselves relatively early in connection with the collections brought from remote and primitive cultures which became the foundation for particular institutions a little before or around the middle of the century.

In the second half and especially towards the end of the century interests in *tradition* asserted themselves in a number of trades and public services in such a way that collections were officially established. This took place first and foremost in the Defence, in the Army and Navy, next in agriculture and fishery and in the first decade of our century came collections, some central, some local, for navigation, whaling and mining, technics, customs, post, police, schools, theatre, etc.

Such interests in tradition gradually widened out, and they have led to the establishment of a very large number of institutions with collections of a more *social-romantic* character. These are the museums that want to show the community's vanishing life-forms, both national, regional and local. The number of country, district and specially registered rural museums is in Norway well over 100. To these must be added a number of village museums, and, naturally, the unifying national institution Norwegian Folk Museum.

Only a handful of these institutions were founded before the turn of the century, so that they really constitute a constantly growing stream in our century, often as a by-product of the simultaneously increasing local historical research and the folkloristic interests.

This growth of institutions after their official founding represents, I believe, as already mentioned, something more than a growing awareness of what is worth taking care of in the museums. The earliest interests, especially the antiquarian and aesthetic interests, have had and will probably continue to have a stronger and perhaps broader public appeal than those based upon the tradition generally in the life-forms. I think it is an important fact to include in the discussions that the things which represent the remote, especially in time, and the aesthetic values in themselves appeal immediately to people without special qualifications and therewith to the political willingness to sacrifice and give priority. Evidence to this effect is the circumstance that these institutions have both funds and technical personnel to a relative extent with which the more recent institutions cannot compare.

But it is in my opinion possible to trace yet another connection between the antiquarian and aesthetic values in relation to the later institutions which are based on social-romantic traditions. These values have in rather a high degree set their stamp on the more recent museums. In the first place the antiquarian stress on origin led, as we know, to restorations, especially of houses which from their functional appearance at the time at which they are dealt with is reconstructed to conform to an "original" state. In the second place, the criteria of choice by which the collections have been made, especially of materials comprising concrete objects, are closely akin to the antiquarian valuations. And in the next place it can scarcely be contestable to assert that much of our older material in the folk museums has a strong list to the aesthetic side.

This may naturally be interpreted to mean that it is the aesthetically valuable materials of concrete object that have been collected by people and therewith been available for the museums to acquire later. But a further consideration is that the art-historical valuations have given stylistic and general aesthetic points of departure for the collection of valuable rather than in the proper sense of the term socially representative objects in the museums. Tendencies away from this have little by little made themselves felt, but it is none the less a circumstance that says a good deal about the museums as a source-foundation for ethnological research.

However, it says more than this. Firstly, it implies, as mentioned earlier, a working basis for those who after being introduced to the discipline find their occupation there. Secondly, the choice of this material will thus set its stamp upon the research interests which are connected with the museums and upon which the discipline in this labour market must build. But thirdly, it is inevitable that also for the future the museums must collect first and last the materials of concrete objects that people believe to be worth collecting, and this on the basis of general social valuations that exclude systematic materials from the contemporary scene.

Here, I think, we have arrived at something of the essential core of the problem of ethnology of the present. For I believe that possibilities of representativeness in the material may shape an ever-clearer basis for the museums' choice of materials by the side of the antiquarian and the aesthetic criteria of choice. But this will scarcely be realized as long as this material is a link in our daily life. These things do not acquire value until they are in process of disappearing, and this situation affects in itself the possibilities of selecting the material. One may collect modern paintings, but hardly modern washing machines.

The conclusion, then, is that as the dominant ethnological labour market, the museums, will scarcely devote themselves to the study of the ethnology of the present to any great extent. I therefore see the study of folk-culture being continued as a predominantly historically oriented science in practice.

Yet this labour market will need research on the present as a basis for the collection of materials when the life-forms are changed. But I believe that the institutions that will do this must be more independent than the museums. It must therefore fall to the lot of the archives and especially the university institutions to be responsible for incorporating the ethnology of the present in its field of activity.

TWO ANALYTICAL PERSPECTIVES IN THE STUDY OF FOLKLIFE

OTTO BLEHR

University of Bergen

IN 1902 an article was published in Sweden on the Finnish colonization in the southern parts of the Scandinavian peninsula (Lönborg, 1902).

This is neither the first nor the last work dealing with this colonization, but, as will be seen from the following, I have a special reason for mentioning this long-forgotten work in connection with our symposium.

The author observes that in the region in question the Swedish settlements are located below the highest marine limit where clays and river sand are deposited. This in contrast to the region above this limit, which consists chiefly of moraine soil. When the Swedes had first cleared the soil they continued to cultivate it year after year. He points out that if one compares economic and geological maps one will generally find that the difference between clay soil and moraine soil coincides with the difference between field and forest.

In contrast to the Swedish settlements he found the Finnish settlements to be located in regions above the highest marine limit. One might expect the reason for this to be that the land below this limit had already been taken by the Swedes. The author points out that this is not the case by showing that the Finns preferred moraine soil for their slash-and-burn farming. This type of agriculture required soil that was drier than the soil in the valleys in order that the trees and bushes cut down would dry enough to burn. Rye and turnips were grown. But what was more important was that from the time when the land was left fallow after the fourth year, and until the forest regained its ascendancy, it gave more abundant hay and better grazing for the domestic animals than would have been available if, like the Swedes, the Finns had had to be content with woodland pasture for their animals. This is an essential point, for from Lönborg's article it seems that we may draw the conclusion that domestic stock was for a long time valued more highly than agriculture by the Finns.

When we know of this evaluation we can from the limitations it imposed explain their decision as regards their choice of location of their dwellings.

In this way the regularity in the pattern of settlement I have sketched above may be explained.

To describe a form and explain how it is generated, is that anything peculiar to Lönborg? Let me answer this question by comparing his work with works by folklife scholars of the historico-geographical school. I will begin with an example which claims to be the first work of this school and which appeared seven years after Lönborg's article (Cederblom, 1909).

In this work the author demonstrates the area of distribution in Sweden for flat, ornamented flax-holders. This region was a strip a few Swedish miles in breadth, and she explains the occurrence of this special type of flax-holder here as a result of diffusion from East Europe. I wish to assert that if one considers an explanation of this type and compares it with Lönborg's explanation of the Finnish pattern of settlement, the last-mentioned mode of explanation is seen to be of a fundamentally different character. To put it bluntly, one may say that Lönborg would have explain-ed the Finnish settlement according to the same principles as Cederblom if he had been content to mention—for this he included too—that it was due to emigration from Finland in the latter half of the sixteenth century and the first half of the seventeenth century. It would not have been neces-sary for him to add that this emigration was a consequence of bad har-vests, war, plundering and near serfdom in Finland, and, on the other hand, encouragement to the Finns from the Swedish State to colonize woodland areas in the central parts of Sweden.

What I wish to emphasize here is that an explanation like that given by Cederblom, which shows only the area of distribution of an object, and explains it as due to contact, is a very inadequate explanation. This is because we do not understand why the variation described occurs. We must also answer the question of *why* flat flax-holders are regarded as so valuable by the population in precisely this region that they want to copy them, whereas this evaluation is not shared by the population outside the region.

More comprehensive than this work by Cederblom is the majority of the other works of the historico-geographical school. They usually include chronologies of the relative age and/or origin of artefacts or other types of cultural manifestations. See, for example, Trotzig's dissertation on "Slagan och andre tröskredskap" (1943). I would assert that also works like these explain little. I do not then consider that they give us chronologies which may be of interest when one is trying to explain technological chan-ges. I will justify this judgement by pointing out that the boundaries for the areas of distribution are here, as for example by Trotzig, explained in terms of "geographical obstacles" or of a "special kind of economic system", or of unverifiable psychological assertions (Trotzig, 1943: 70 ff.; see also Svensson, 1966: 69 ff.).

It may be argued that it is not fair to criticize the investigations of the historico-geographical school because these were never meant to be anything but groundwork, and that the investigations have not yet been developed to the stage where their results can be seriously judged (Erixon, 1950–1: 7). To this I will reply that when scholars have not yet after half a century proved the legitimacy of their methods they must expect to be criticized.

The most fruitful point at which to level criticism is their use of the culture concept. From their works it emerges that they look upon material artefacts and "customs" as culture elements, and that they treat them analytically on the same level as the conceptions lying behind these manifestations. One also gets the feeling that culture "lives" a "life" independently of the individuals in the community. It is as if the individuals only have to conform to the norms and rules their culture sets up for them. See, for example, Kolsrud: "... (cultural phenomena are) the learned behaviour that the community has approved of as right" (1961–3: 293), and Stigum: "... people live and work in a milieu in which there is a host of usages and customs that control and decide the way of life of the people,... (1961: 63: 345). This view of culture must be based on an assumption that there is a necessary functional/moral connection between all the artefacts studied and the "customs" of which the cultures consist. This connection makes the culture "right" for the individuals, or makes it impossible for them not to do "what they are supposed to do".

With such a mechanical view of culture it is not necessary for scholars of this school to look at social life in order to understand how cultural forms are maintained. Material objects and "customs" can be studied independently of the social context in which they appear.

Where it is a matter of investigations of local communities I have a feeling that they believe they have proved—on this local level—the usefulness of the method by describing the local community as a functional unit. But in works of this type too we get no understanding of the relationship between the elements studied and of how the form described is generated.

I am of the opinion that this way of regarding culture, with its unfortunate methodological and theoretical consequences, is largely responsible for the crisis in which folklife research as a science finds itself today.

I shall try in the following to show how we, with an alternative view of culture, can emerge from this crisis.

Let me revert to Lönborg's work. What makes the analysis valuable is that the author—even if not explicitly—takes as his point of departure an evaluation by the Finns and shows how it generates the regular pattern of settlement he has found.

We find a complete development of such a theoretical approach in Barth (1966). He regards the regularities in social behaviour as a result of the rational choices made by individuals in their efforts to attain particular goals. If one accepts this view, then the regularities observed can no longer be treated as "customs", they are statistical patterns in human behaviour. It then becomes natural to look for the social process that generates the regularity observed. We must, in other words, ask what are the factors which encourage the particular individual, for example a farmer or a crofter, to make particular decisions in the specific situation in which he finds himself. The observed regularities in social life must then be a result of a sharing of the most important values by the individuals; this is to say that they share the same cultural notions. When in a society one finds differences in behaviour leading to different groupings, this may be understood as a result of differences in the individuals' resources and possibilities, and it becomes our task to reveal these differences.

I will illustrate what has been said above by showing the impact of this new view of culture on the study of folk beliefs. This research at first aimed at a charting of the elements of which each belief-notion was composed. I may here mention Faye's (1833 and 1843) important works where he analyses supernatural beings in Nordic folk belief and shows the different elements of which each notion is composed.

In more recent times psychological explanations have here increasingly come to dominate (see, for example, Granberg, 1935; Solheim, 1939; Eskeröd, 1947, Honko, 1964; Tillhagen, 1965). The psychological explanations at which these scholars have arrived may on paper appear more or less reasonable, but as they are unverifiable they must be considered to be of no scientific value. To give an example: Granberg asserts in the article to which I have referred that the element of folk belief concerning erotic wood nymphs is a result of sexual fantasies in lonely woodsmen (Granberg, 1935: 229).

A more profitable point of departure for the study of folk beliefs is to take these notions for *granted*, and rather to concentrate on the main characteristica of the communication of folk beliefs.

I have recently done this (Blehr, 1965 and 1967) and found that a story-teller, whenever telling a story, used the same folk belief elements. I also found that folk belief stories based on the same specific event can become independent stories for story-tellers in different local communities. Finally I found that it was essential for the story-teller to be able to vouch for the trustworthiness of the person who had had the experience. The story-teller achieved this either by himself vouching for the protagonist, or by telling his audience that the person from whom he had heard the story had vouched for him. As a consequence the folk belief stories did not have more than, at the most, two intermediate links between the protagonist and the recipient.

If now we ask why this regular pattern in the folk belief stories emerges the explanation is found in the circumstance that the stories must be communicated as if they were true. This obliges a story-teller to take care that his variants do not contradict each other, as he cannot avoid that persons in his community will hear him tell the same story on several occasions. On the other hand, when a folk belief story becomes part of the repertoire of a story-teller from another local community, the story may be communicated by him with a different content. This does not matter as the new story-teller in his local community will have another audience. This new audience will rarely be able to question the truth of the particular version they hear by comparing it with other variants of the same story.

The reason for entering into such detail with this example is that I want to illustrate how this alternative view of culture explains regularities in the phenomena we are studying. Because this explanatory model is based on social behaviour it may be falsified by empirical evidence. It thus differs on an essential point from the unverifiable psychological explanations set forth by scholars of the historico-geographical school.

From what I have here asserted it should become apparent that I clearly dissociate myself from the historico-geographical school in Nordic folklife research. I maintain that we can only arrive at an understanding of the regularities observed with a conception of culture other than the one which researchers of this school have.

Let me at this point underline what this alternative conception of culture implies methodologically. If we consider my analysis of the form of the folk belief stories it will be seen that it is by making the social context relevant that I can explain how cultural values find expression as observed regularity in form.

Thus, the social context in which the phenomena we study are embedded becomes essential for our analysis. If we, to give just one more example, ask how the folk belief notions are maintained, I postulate that it is essential for their maintenance that their elements are expressed in stories with a contemporary frame of reference. This explanation must also be empirically verifiable if it is to be anything but a postulate.

Thanks to historical data it has been possible for me to show that the social situation at the time when the folk belief notions were generally held was precisely as I have asserted. A quotation from Asbjörnsen concerning his visit in Hedalen in 1847 will illustrate this: " . . . my harvest consisted chiefly of legends *(sagn)* and folk belief stories *(huldreeventyr)*; these were not only from grandfather's and father's youth, but from the year before, from last year, when the dairy maids were the last time in the mountains, from last winter and from last spring, when the men were out shooting or getting loads of leaves and moss in the woods and on the mountain" (1964: 12–13).

The most important problem with which we are confronted when working with reconstructions of this type is that the social process resulting in the described form can no longer be deduced from observations. We are therefore dependent for our explanation of cultural forms on historical sources of three types: printed narratives, artefacts, or oral material from individuals who once shared the evaluations that were expressed in these forms. Of these sources the last-mentioned is the most important. It is also the most demanding, as the information we seek about cultural evaluations our informants have had, and the social situation in which they found themselves, cannot emerge as answers to a questionnaire. It is only through patient interviews and by building up confidence between informant and investigator that one may hope little by little to get the knowledge necessary for a reconstruction.

I have myself completed a rather comprehensive work of this kind on the basis of interviews in Sörkedalen, which was a small feudal settlement in Oslo. In my study I show how the social organization in the last quarter of the nineteenth century may be understood as a result of the formal labour organization in which the estate management instructed the workers to take part, and the private arrangements the workers could find within this frame (Blehr, 1961). I think that in this work I have been able to give a relatively rich picture of the traditional social organization in the valley. In spite of this I maintain that the picture would have been much richer if I had been able to base my investigations on contemporary observations. For even the fullest information the best informant can give of social life as it has once been can only be a shadow of what we ourselves would have been able to observe.

In a number of works (Blehr, 1963, 1964, 1966 and MS.) I have elaborated this statement. On the basis of my own observations I explain regularities in social organization in the Faroe Islands by showing how a central valuation held by the Faroe Islanders is made relevant for the decision they make in the various social situations in which they find themselves. I arrived at an understanding of this evaluation through intensive fieldwork in *one* local community. I wish to emphasize the importance of the local community as a point of departure for the collection of data, even if this has emerged implicitly in my examples in the foregoing.

From these examples it is clear that the organizational frame of social life is first and foremost the local community. It is within the possibilities and limitations this defines for the individuals that regularities in their behaviour are generated taking into account their evaluations. When these evaluations are known one can explain the form social life has in the local community investigated, and by working in other local communities discover whether these evaluations are specific or general. In this way one can gradually extend the investigation and arrive at an understanding of social life within larger entities.

What also makes such contemporary investigations so fruitful is that regularities in social behaviour not employed to arrive at the explanatory model may at a later stage of the investigation be used to control the model. On the Faroe Islands, for example, I at first realized that the kinship obligations that I had revealed through the composition of working groups on land as well could explain the recruiting of large and small boatcrews. Later on I discovered that the same evaluation could also explain regularities in demographic mobility and political groupings, both on the local and on the central level.

In my examples I have moved from the forms of the folk belief stories found in the pre-industrial society to political groupings in a modern industrial society. By choosing these examples it is my hope that I have been able to illustrate the breadth which the new view on culture can give to folklife research.

Such a view makes meaningless the typological distinction of folk culture in contrast to other cultures. Folk culture, as I see it, are the notions which are shared by the individuals in an area. This area may be more or less regional.

From the views I here maintain it may be seen that I regard folklife research as a science whose task is to describe and explain how the notions shared by an ethnic group find expression through a social process in cultural forms.

What justifies us in choosing Scandinavia as our field of work is that, despite regional variations, we share most of the fundamental values and, for subjective reasons, regarded an understanding of these essential.

Our science is, in other words, regional. It is this that makes us different from social anthropologists, although I think we must accept the consequences of the theoretical viewpoints that are developed in that discipline. Our task—in contrast to that of the social anthropologist, who works comparativ ely—is to describe and explain the form our Nordic society has, and has had, in the *greatest possible detail*.

On the basis of the theoretical view I have sketched here, one can work with reconstructions of how conditions were at an earlier time, or attempt to understand the society of today. One should only realize that the result will be more or less rewarding depending on the techniques one has at one's disposal for the collection of data.

We also have a responsibility to our folk museums. These must, to a greater extent than in the case today, stop being technological and typological churchyards over artefacts and folkart from our pre-industrial Nordic society. What we as scholars can do to alter this is to show the implications for the exhibitions in our museums of the fact that the values individuals share through a *social process in local communities* give rise to the cultural forms we can observe. This view implies that the showing of milieus must be the essential thing for our museums. To make these milieu-studies alive we must put the majority of the artefacts back in the store-rooms. Instead, with the help of visual aids, such as models and dioramas, we must try to the best of our ability to show the social and ecological possibilities and limitations that constitute the individuals' universe in the local communities we are describing.

Such milieus may then be supplemented with survey exhibitions showing the main features in cultural and ecological variations within the regions of Scandinavia which the different museums see it as their task to cover.

Let me in conclusion explain why I have restricted my criticism to works by Nordic researchers of the historico-geographic school only. As a Nordic folklife researcher I have found this restriction natural, for even if I know that the same criticism might also be directed against folklife researchers on the Continent and ethnographers (anthropologists) of the same school, it is with the conditions in Scandinavia that I am best acquainted.

Hammarstedt said once that "only thoughtlessness passes judgement on the past in terms of his own time". I should like to make his words my own by saying that it is my hope that my criticism will not be taken personally. I fully realize that the scholars who have worked in the historico-geographic school have, considered their time and their theoretical background, done important work. But science has developed further, and we in our time must be willing to open up for these new impulses.

It is my hope that by suggesting an alternative to the traditional direction my criticism may be such an impulse. Just as I found shortcomings in the school that dominated the discipline when I entered it, others will certainly find shortcomings in the approach I am advocating. But in the meantime I will maintain that these views have a fruitful place in our discipline.

REFERENCES

ASBJÖRNSEN, P. CHR. (1964) "Indberetning om en Reise, foretagen med Understöttelse af Universitetets Stipendiefond i Sommeren 1847, for at samle Folkedigtninger, Eventyr, Sagn, Viser etc., etc.", in Tradisjonsinssamling på 1800-talet, *Norsk Folkeminnelags skrifter 92*, Oslo.
BARTH, F. (1966) Models of social organization, *JRAI, Occasional Paper No. 23*, London.
BLEHR, O. (1961) Sosiale implikasjoner av den tradisjonelle arbeidsorganisasjon i Sörkedalen, *Norveg VII*, Oslo.
BLEHR, O. (1963) Action Groups in a Society with Bilateral Kinship: A Case Study from the Faroe Islands, *Ethnology*, Vol. 2, No. 3, Pittsburgh.
BLEHR, O. (1964) Ecological Change and Organizational Continuity in the Faroe Islands, *Folk*, Vol. 6, Part 1, Copenhagen.
BLEHR, O. (1965) Noen synspunkter på analysen av folketrofortellinger, *Etnografisk Museums Årsbok 1965*, Oslo.
BLEHR, O. (1966) Samtidsobservasjoner i folkelivsforskningen belyst med eksempler fra Faeröyene. (Lecture at the 17th Nordic folklife Researchers' Congress in Falun, 966. *Stencilled.*)
BLEHR, O. (1967) The Analysis of Folk Belief Stories and its Implications for Research on Folk Belief and Folk Prose, *Fabula*, Vol. 9, Berlin.
BLEHR, O. (MS.) Social Organization of the Faroese Islanders.
CEDERBLOM, G. (1909) Några af våra äldsta spånadsredskap och deras ättlingar, *Fataburen*, 1909, Stockholm.
ERIXON, S. (1950–1) An introduction to Folklife Research or Nordic Ethnology. *Folkliv*, Vols. XIV–XV, Stockholm.
ESKERÖD, A. (1947) Årets äring, *Nordiska Museets Handlingar 26*, Stockholm.
FAYE, A. (1833 and 1843) Norske Folke-Sagn (here after: *Norsk Folkeminnelags Skrifter 63*, Oslo, 1948).
GRANBERG, G. (1935) Skogsrået i yngre nordisk folktradition, *Skrifter utgivna av Kungliga Gustav Adolfs Akademien for Folklivsforskning 3*, Uppsala.
HONKO, L. (1964) Memorates and the Study of Folk Beliefs, *Journal of the Folklore Institute*, Vol. 1, No. 1/2, Bloomington.
KOLSRUD, K. (1961–3) Etnologi, Sosiologi og lokalhistorie, *Heimen*, Oslo.
LÖNBORG, S. (1902) Finnmarkerna i mellersta Skandinavien, *Ymer*, Stockholm.
SOLHEIM, S. (1939) Ålmene fordomar ved fiske, *Ord og sed*, Oslo.
STIGUM, H. (1961–3) Etnologien som universitetsfag og garden som etnologisk forskningsfelt, *Heimen*, Oslo.
SVENSSON, S. (1966) *Introduktion till Folklivsforskning*, Stockholm.
TILLHAGEN, C. H. (1965) Gruvskrock, *Norveg XII*, Oslo.
TROTZIG, D. (1943) Slagan och andra tröskredskap, *Nordiska Museets Handlingar 17*, Stockholm.

URBAN ETHNOLOGY AND RESEARCH ON THE PRESENT

Sven B. Ek

Institute of Ethnology, University of Lund

Now that the eventual orientation of ethnology towards research on the present has been taken up for discussion the question of the relation to urban ethnology naturally comes into the picture. The relation between urban ethnology and the ethnology of the present is the subject for this contribution, which should be seen as a personal declaration based on my own experience and my own view of ethnology.

The concept urban ethnology is probably as a rule understood as a synonym for the actually more adequate designation ethnology of the built-up area. The problems it is here intended to study are seldom specific for the town proper, but refer as a rule to small market-towns and built-up areas without administrative boundaries. At the same time, however, there are in reality at least to a certain extent different premises for the shaping of folk-culture in the town and in types of community comparable with the town on the one hand and the administratively dependent built-up areas on the other hand. The difference lies above all in the degree in which central administration plays a role. But the practical reasons are all in favour of our acceptance of the term urban ethnology as a synonym with a wider import, since, for one thing, the concept town in the sense of built-up area in general is already used in both the Swedish and Anglo-Saxon social sciences –I will not here attempt to discuss the definition of built-up area, which is of no particular interest to us at present –now strictly speaking, neither the ethnology of the built-up area nor urban ethnology are very happily chosen terms, as they express only the spatial aspect of research. *In et per se*, the concepts are equally applicable to studies of today's community and studies of the community of the eighteenth century. But as regards the object of research, the material and the methods employed, the difference between the two cases is very great. It is on the whole probably the case that the study of the pre-industrial town is closer to the ethnology with a traditional slant than to the research on the built-up area which concentrates on the community in the industrial era. It is probably also true that those agitating for ethnological urban studies have in general had the built-up areas of the industrial era in mind. The opposition between tradition-oriented ethnology and the projected urban ethnology has, I think, lain as much on the social and chronological as on the spatial planes.

There are practical, methodological and theoretical reasons why also linguistically one should distinguish between the urban ethnology dealing with the present and that dealing with the pre-industrial community. It ought then to be possible to use the term urban ethnology of the researches on built-up areas in the industrial community. For other periods preindustrial may be a suitable summarizing prefix. I shall in the following leave pre-industrial urban ethnology on one side.

Now it is clear, however, that urban ethnology, with the delimitation of the concept that I have found desirable, is only a part of a wider research-field that I should like to call ethnology of the present in contradistinction to the tradition-oriented ethnology. A concept like the present is, of course, in itself very dubious. Not only because the time-import is necessarily in a state of flux, but also because the backward limit is diffuse. But unless by ethnology of the present is to be meant some kind of "just-now" research or we are to lapse into pure arbitrariness, the best limit-zone is in this case given: the time around 1870 when the development of industrialization and urbanization gathered speed and the *premisses* of the tradition-bound peasant culture were palpably changed. I thus see urban ethnology as a sub-concept to the ethnology of the present; the term specifies location in space and community types. The potential problem-complex in the ethnology of the present must to a large extent be common to both the urban and the rural community. But different types of community naturally also constitute different objects of research; it may be a consequence of the practical just as well as of the structural circumstances. The resemblances to which the historically conditioned research conditions, concrete or otherwise, give rise are, however, undoubtedly more numerous and significant than the differences which may arise from the community difference.

The question of the relation of urban ethnology to morphological urban research cannot be completely passed by in this connection. The term urban ethnology may appear to be the most adequate for an ethnological investigation of the town as a functional entity. The object of such an investigation would, certainly, not be the so-called folk-life, but rather what one may call the abstractions of the urban community. An orientation towards something purely theoretical would not of course, *per se*, be a bad thing. But there is a decisive objection both to the attempt to form an ethnological research with this aim and to the reservation of the term urban ethnology for this. Morphological urban research is, as we know, a field which has been cleared and which is still being cultivated by both sociologists and human-geographers—under different names. And it is not the job of ethnology to perpetuate or to contribute to a greater, confusion of concepts, but to add to the sum of knowledge from its own points of departurte. But to avoid misunderstandings I will make a point of stressing that I do not consider morphological urban research to be irrelevant for urban ethnology. Ecological investigations are, for example, often necessary both for the posing and the solving of ethnological problems; but they should constitute rather a method than a goal for us.

What, then, is to be the research-object of urban ethnology? One makes it easiest for oneself by saying that in principle urban ethnology need not differ from the ethnology which aims at the study of the tradition-bound peasant community, that it covers material and social culture as well as popular belief and folklore. It may be said, I think, that this attitude set its stamp upon, for example, Ulma's urban questionnaires, which were used especially in connection with the nation-wide collections in the 1940's. It was found, however, that generation of informants and the milieus that were reached were too young, and the results were relatively meagre. In their endeavour to reach the solidly traditional the questionnaires were better suited for the pre-industrial than for the industrial urban community with its great mobility. Even if one can accept the thesis of the theoretical similarity between urban and tradition-oriented ethnology as a general declaration, it is clear that the differences in reality must be considerable. This is soon found if one analyses the significance of the material culture for urban and tradition-oriented ethnology respectively.

The function of the material culture-elements in the community, the interaction, for instance, between object and social behaviour, between dwelling area and dwelling habits—that is the material culture-element as part of the social and psychological pattern should now be our object. In urban ethnology one ought, in other words, to try to subordinate the research trends that were formerly, in practice, more or less independent, to a common goal in which the social behaviour is what is central.

The ideal research object for urban ethnology, as for all ethnology, might be summarized in three concepts: culture-pattern, social structure, change. Not the elementary, but the complicated, not the static, but the dynamic, not the unique, but the typical.

One of the three components of the ideal research object is thus change. But this, too, is not a new aspect; it is this that has made and still makes ethnology a historical science. Also the ethnologists who play with the idea of being able to make a prognostic science out of ethnology must admit that the historical analysis must precede the setting up to deterministic schemata.

But this is not to say that the ethnologist must constantly have recourse to a remembered material. One possibility which is one of the main questions for this symposium is to collect current material which might later— of course duly analysed—be followed up with corresponding investigations at later dates. Also in this case, however, as far as I can understand, the *final* synthesis will be made from an historical perspective, even if one does not strive to follow the sequence of the development. The futuristic collection of data and the futuristic research model—if I can use the terms without being misunderstood—presupposes, however, that one has a good knowledge of and is able clearly to define one's research object. This may today be possible in rural ethnology, but scarcely in urban ethnology. In the present situation I think it is clear that the futuristic line must as regards urban ethnology step back for the historical line.

But the two research lines have a point of intersection, viz. our own day and time. For both it holds true that it is there the base material can be collected; it is probably chiefly from here that the problems will be posed, whether they can afterwards be solved with a comparative historical or futuristic material.

It may seem that this statement is at variance with the views I have earlier propounded in my articles in *Folkliv* (1964–5) and Rig (1966). What I pointed out in the article was that in urban ethnology I saw not a new, but a continuative science. That is to say, a further development, in the industrial era, of the investigation of the process of culture transformation already begun in the peasant community. That in this connection I particularly stressed the first stages of industrialization in the built-up community did not, however, imply a declaration in principle that precisely that period was of unique interest. My motivation is in the first place that ethnology as an historical science has not the right to make jumps in time, more especially where it is a matter of periods that one actually can reach, even if it costs a little effort. And in the second place that one has here the possibility of studying an acculturation process rather closely, and this is, of course, a research which is of great theoretical interest and for which ethnology is especially well equipped. As a consequence of this I have recommended that our resources for the collection of material should for the time being be directed not towards our own time but towards the early stages of industrialism. We shall otherwise lose the interview material necessary for research, and therewith also the possibilities of studying these stages. Thus the points of view I have developed are not so much the theoretical as the practical.

In the investigations of the early stages of industrialization I therefore see a task of very present, not to say urgent, interest for urban ethnology. But for those who still carry the remains of an early acquired culture- and social-anthropological ballast the ideal for ethnology of the present seems by no means to be to concentrate attention always on the past and, unfortunately, from the point of view of materials, always less easily graded periods. Ethnology has often boasted of its will to study Man. Nowhere has one better possibilities of collecting material for such a study than in one's own time. Only through field-studies of the present has one the complete possibilities of complementing and differentiating one's observations. And for the ethnologist it can in any case scarcely be more unimportant to try to grasp his own times than earlier stages.

Contemporary studies are thus just as important a task for urban ethnology as for any other ethnology of the present. But here I must confess to my dogmatic irresponsibility. It is easy enough to say that one must give an account of Man in the present. But it is not equally easy to do this—and especially not if one wants to retain ethnology's hard-earned special character. We ought, certainly, to apply the ideal aim also to research on the present, but I do not think that it is strictly in accordance with this that we should begin our study. Let us instead ask ourselves where we can just now work with the greatest profit. And this has a certain connection with our knowledge of earlier stages in the industrial and even pre-industrial community. In question here is especially one field, a sector of folk-life where we have possibilities of arriving at a result; I am referring here to the investigation of today's religious conceptions, valuations and norms, what one may call the dominants of the social structure and the culture pattern.

The point of departure for an urban ethnology with this aim must, of course, be a thorough knowledge of the study-object in today's community and culture. The foundation is constituted by collections of data and observations in the field, and the first scientific goal is to see the chosen attitude or attitudes in their functional context. But as ethnologists we have therewith, in my opinion, only gone half of the way. The attitude is the product not only of the function, but also of its historical context. And a number of conceptions are to be designated rather as functionless relics if they can still be fitted into their personal and social pattern.

The historical aspect is what in my opinion ought to characterize ethnological is contradistinction, for example, to sociological urban research. If we surrender this, there is a great risk of the subject's being lost, even if it remains in name. This view is not merely an expression for a scientific traditionalism; it is based on the conviction that no community, no period can be fully understood without our knowing the historical background. Without the historical insight one can get to know the character, function and *visible* motives of the pattern or structure, but not all the *invisible* motives. If one accepts this thesis and considers that the historically conditioned cause—as a part of the mutability—is one of ethnology's primary goals, one must also—to revert to what I have touched upon above—in the name of consistency realize the necessity of taking up the neglected collection of material relating to the community of early industrialism. It is in the lacunae of our knowledge that we can find the answers to many of the questions our own time can pose.

It is thus not only ethnology's duty as an historical science that requires the discipline to turn now to the community of industrialism from and including its beginning—it is also a necessary prerequisite for the ethnological research on the present of the type I have here described.

But even if one sees the relatively long period of time as a research-unit and should wish to study the development as a continuum, one must bow to actual and practical circumstances. The sequence of a train of thought can rarely be followed historically without interruptions and perhaps lateral excursions. The continuity in an historical observation cannot be more than the researcher's dream. But if the ideal method is unattainable, there is nevertheless a next best way which seems practicable; one might say that it is the futuristic research model though in reverse. Instead of trying to collect the material with time intervals forwards and analysing, one can do this backwards. In this way we should get the necessary fixed points of reference for our observations of the course and the connection. With common time-targets one would probably also arrive at a broad knowledge of the culture-forms of the different points of time, that is, at least partly meet also the requirements which may be made on ethnology as an historically descriptive science.

Here, however, I must link up with one of my earlier definitions. According to the programme sketched here one would thus try to select suitable points of time to which the intensive investigations might be bound. But a first question is *which* points of time? Is one to choose those which have special significance for the general development? It is not so sure that these are the best. Ethnological time and historical time are different real phenomena. When I chose the period about 1870 as a limit backwards for the ethnology of the present this was an historically motivated drawing of a line that I can for the time being accept for practical reasons. However, I am very doubtful whether one should refer to this period as an ethnological boundary zone. In several local investigations I have, on the contrary, as regards the peasant community had occasion to criticize the notion of the great ethnological importance of the point of time. The ethnological time-division should, of course, not be based so much on certain outer culture changes as on structural changes, permutations of the thinking and the norms.

It may probably be taken as a general rule that the historical events which provide the conditions for changes in the social structure really take effect relatively late, as they must act as it were, within the frame of the "set" or fixed social structure. As a general historical one can note decisions and their outer realization, one can record the first appearance and political victory of the ideas. But the ethnologist's task is to follow the integration of the new with the social structure, and this does not take place on the day when a decision is arrived at or a meeting has made a declaration. I will take an example from my investigations in Nöden in Lund. As early as the end of the nineteenth century active Social Democracy in Lund have launched an attack on Church and clergy. The poor workers living in Nöden about 1900 were loyal Social Democrats but they were also in general loyal to the Established Church, even if they seldom *went* to church. People clung stubbornly to the church confirmation and were rather indifferent than negative to the clergy. The class struggle slogans had not yet gained a hold; the current attitude to the so-called rich was far from being characterized by hate or even aversion. The attitude-pattern at which I have arrived is on the whole still that of the rural common people. The result indicates that the changes in attitude did not take place until after the 1910's.

My point is thus that we should try to take our cross-sections at dates which are significant not in the first place for current history but for ethnology. And from this follows— unfortunately—a weakening of the projected research program. A good many "point"-investigations are needed before one knows where the cross-sections may best be taken. If it were possible, it would undoubtedly be best if these "point"-studies could have been fitted into a system of encirclement. But I am doubtful of the possibilities of carrying this out with the present resources of ethnology. This gives me occasion once more to stress the advisability of letting urban ethnology run with a free rein to begin with. It is better to wait and see and to build upon the results of a free research than perhaps to be obliged to constate that a directed research has been aimed not only at the wrong target, but also at the wrong time.

My stressing of the importance of the possible for the shaping of urban ethnology makes it incumbent upon me to say something of the material we may have to do with. Can one really carry on an historical research on attitudes on the basis of remembered material? In this point the majority are thrown back upon preconceived opinions in the one or other direction. I will immediately make a reservation on the basis of my own experience. We do not arrive at finely differentiated views; the general trends must be our target.

But apart from this. Can one rely on the candour and trustworthiness of the subjects interviewed? As regards the first question I must rely upon my own view. In the worker population in Lund and Eslöv, at least, the questioning so far carried out has been answered with an evident candidness that is surprising. It would seem that the informants' time-distance has been a favourable factor for the questioning. Nor must it be forgotten that the interviews have hitherto been held in a milieu in which social conventions have not played a very inhibiting role. In other connections I have as an example pointed to the candour in the matters of hygiene and alcohol habits in the subjects' own childhood homes, and this is an example that speaks strongly in favour of the material.

The trustworthiness of the material is not, however, dependent on the character of the individual interview. However decided and detailed an interview may be, it may be atypical for the group or even directly misleading. But it is, of course, not on the single data that we base our conclusions. Ethnology has striven to base the scientific observations on large materials, where it is only the unanimity that permits of the conclusion. Quantitatively satisfactory materials and clear statistical results may naturally be got as well from interviews based on recollection as on others. And there is scarcely reason to assume that the sources of error will be more numerous or greater than in interviews on current attitudes. It is not the memory-material itself, but the personnel resources for its collection that are decisive for the question as to whether an historical research on attitudes is possible or not. Let me here add as an obvious fact in passing that one must try to correlate the interview material with other suitable material where such exists. In my as yet unpublished investigation on Nöden in Lund I have, for instance, in certain points made use of a comprehensive statistico-demographic material as a check on the attitude picture the interviews have given.

I will here only briefly touch upon the methods for the collection of material. Ethnology has up to now been working extensively, through the academic institutions and museums. Regional or national collections have been made by the permanently employed information staff. The charting of the culture areas may here probably be said to be the research-historical motivation. This type of collecting is not in very good odour today; many think it has served its purpose. I myself do not share this view; on the contrary, it would be a good thing if the organization with the suppliers of information could be extended also to the towns. But it is at the same time indisputable that the material got through the unschooled local suppliers of information is inadequate for many research aims. It is, for example, perfectly obvious that it has a limited value in itself for studies of the social structure. The local intensive investigations, which afford greater possibilities of observing both the whole and the dynamism, must therefore constitute the methodical foundation of urban ethnology. Through these one often has the possibility of interpreting the extensive surface material and extracting more of its potential content. I will especially emphasize that the local intensive investigation should be utilized not only in connection with contemporary studies. It is equally important that it should be used in the retrospective research, and there in a form as little modified as possible.

There is thus in my opinion every reason to have a positive view of the bearing power of the memory-material. It makes it possible for us to establish at different dates—back to about 1890—individual attitudes and presumably also to chart social structures rather satisfactorily. By this, however, I by no means wish to assert that the specific ethnological material can supply the solutions to all our questions. The ability to do so depends on the nature of the problems. I will exemplify this with some problems and sketches.

In any case in the older generation there are many people also in the towns who are very afraid of landing up in hospital. This is a feeling which may perhaps enter in a certain personal pattern, but it can scarcely be fitted in functionally in a social or cultural pattern. There can be no doubt but that we have here to do with a kind of attitude-fixation. It is the same fear as we earlier find instanced in the traditional material. The notion that one was practically dead if one landed up in hospital has obviously been common formerly, at least in the country districts. And in reality there was a certain justification for this notion. The hospital mortality was high. This in its turn has doubtless been connected with the belier in quacks and old-fashioned home-cures combined with a not altogether unmotivated disparagement of the medical corps; this meant that people would often not entrust themselves to the hospital until they were lost beyond saving. One finds a connection between the attitude of that day, the insufficient number of doctors, the ignorance in the pre-industrial community and—not least important—the social structure of the peasant community.

In this case, as far as I can see, the solutions lie within the immediate reach of ethnology. One may take another example of great topical interest. It is often seen that when in a tight spot policemen seldom get help from the public If the citizenry does not turn direct against the police and take the part of an intoxicated trouble-maker, it is in any case not unusual for bystanders to feel more sympathy for the disturber of the peace than for the party protecting this. The negative attitude to the police belong doubtless among the historically conditioned attitudes, and is nowadays in a way unmotivated. Now I cannot pretend to give an explanation for the origin of the phenomenon. I might, however, venture to suggest hypothetically that we have here to do with a pronounced town-custom, that there is here a very ancient connection with the attitude to night-watchmen and similar functionaries with the duty of keeping order, but that the social conditions prevailing at the turn of the century and the symbolizing of the class society by the police may have played a great role. Through observations and chartings of our own time we might ascertain the functional intensity of the attitude and its distribution in different social groups and types of community. Through the memory-material we might follow the attitude back in time and get to know its motivation or what people believed and believe to be its motivation. But if my hypothesis is right we shall not arrive at a correct view without a thorough historical knowledge and depth-studies in the history of social valuations.

Space does not permit me to adduce more examples, but it is otherwise not difficult to point to ethnological research problems where our science must go outside its own sector of materials. I have in another connection described ethnology as a synthetic science, and this is something which ought to apply in a particularly high degree to urban ethnology and to all other ethnologies of the present. If urban ethnology is to be successful, the ethnologist must have a broad historical knowledge, and he must also have thoroughly acquainted himself with the view of method and goal held in the nearly allied social sciences. But it would be arrogant to believe that synthetic ethnology can in all matters manage by itself. To reach its goals and still be ethnology it must seek help and collaboration.

My reflections on urban ethnology and the ethnology of the present lead me finally to the conclusion that the alignment of research is a strong imperative for us at last to try to realize the transverse-scientific collaboration which so many desire but which it is evidently so difficult to realize.

COMPARATIVE MILIEU STUDIES. SOME TOPICAL POINTS OF VIEW

ALBERT ESKERÖD

The Nordiska Museet, Stockholm

WITHOUT going into the many designations the subject has had and in part still has, I here use the terms ethnology and cultural anthropology as equivalent. On the other hand, I understand the designation "social anthropology" especially cherished by Radcliffe-Brown as constituting only a limited part of the field of ethnology or cultural anthropology. For both of these terms, moreover, it seems possible through the qualifications "general" or "regional" to indicate a more comprehensive or a limited part of the subject. How the regional qualification is to be applied will naturally depend on the end in view. Swedish ethnology thus constitutes a part of the general European ethnology. European ethnology, on the other hand, is of course limited in relation to a general, global ethnology.

These points of view may naturally seem very elementary, but the confused thicket of terms that are still used as a designation for the subject shows that it may be important really to know what one is speaking about.

Nordic ethnology is today much more influenced by the new trends, especially in British and American cultural anthropology, than it was about 20 years ago. Even if researchers like Franz Boas, R. H. Lowie, A. L. Kroeber, F. C. Bartlett and C. D. Ford began to become known, the field was for the most part dominated by the historical school. Ruth Benedict was even earlier in a way a harbinger with her literary and elegant presentation of the new culture-holistic viewpoints. Little attention was paid to A. V. Radcliffe-Brown and Bronislav Malinowski, and their sharply formulated theses met for a long time with stubborn and in part unjust resistance. One of the reasons for this was that functionalism was accused of being anti-historical, at the same time as it was emphatically asserted that occidental ethnology must be an historical science. Nothing, surely, can be more self-evident than this last-mentioned view—so self-evident, in fact, that it is scarcely in need of special mention. As regards the anti-historical attitude of the so-called functionalists, one does not need to read many pages of their writings in order to refute this completely erroneous, but prejudiced and slightly complacent statement. I will here only quote some lines from Radcliffe-Brown and Malinowski.

Even as early as the year 1923, it is true, Radcliffe-Brown finds the difference between historical study and his own programme so essential that he wants to refer to them with completely different names, so that the first-mentioned school is designated as "ethnology—the historical method, which explains a given institution or complex of institutions by tracing the stages of its development and finding wherever possible the particular cause or occasion of each change that has taken place"—while he wants "to use the term social anthropology as the name of the study that seeks to formulate the general laws that underlie the phenomena of culture" (1923, pp. 125, 127).

Nearly 30 years later Radcliffe-Brown writes the following (1952, p. 186):

> Similarly one "explanation" of a social system will be its history where we know it, the detailed account of how it came to be what it is and where it is. Another "explanation" of the same system is obtained by showing (as the functionalist attempts to do) that it is a special exemplification of laws of social physiology or social functioning. The two kinds of explanation do not conflict, but supplement one another.

The criticism applies here, of course, also to the historical reconstructions without sufficient source-material. The whole of Malinowski's theory of science, not least as it has been summarized in *A Scientific Theory of Culture and other Essays* (1944, pp. 175 f.), is leavened by an historical view of the development of culture. He says here, moreover, summarizing his views:

> Functionalism, I would like to state emphatically, is hostile neither to the study of distribution, nor to the reconstruction of the past in terms of evolution, history or diffusion. It only insists that unless we define cultural phenomena in function as well as in form, we may be led into such fantastic evolutionary schemes as those of Morgan, Bachofen or Engels, or to piecemeal treatments of isolated items, such as those of Frazer, Briffault and even Westermarck. Again, if the student of distributions maps out fictitious and unreal similarities, his labors will be wasted. Thus functionalism definitely insists that as a preliminary analysis of culture it has its fundamental validity, and that it supplies the anthropologist with the only valid criteria of cultural identification.

A relatively new trend in Nordic ethnology, at least in Sweden, is, as we know, that we have shifted the time-limit for investigations and research nearer to the present, not to say in direct contact with the present. If this had not been the case, we should after all not have had occasion to come together here to a symposium on the ethnology of the present.

This moving forward of the time-limit naturally applies also to the documentation of the cultural transformation which lies in the collection of objects and which, of course, in the first place concerns the central museums in the culture-historical field. And in the Nordic Museum we have for many years been engaged in this task, even if—it must be admitted— certain external circumstances and lack of financial resources has prevented this work from becoming as comprehensive as is motivated. Nor, as a matter of fact, are we yet quite in a position to say how this documentation of more recent development is best to be compassed with the help of all the new methods of documentation available, and in the face of the tremendous variety the cultural inventory represents. We are here faced with very difficult decisions, and unfortunately at present practically without the financial resources for necessary work outside the office.

This shifting of the time-limit for the target for investigations and research makes it a still more urgent desideratum than before that boundary-lines and possibilities of collaboration with neighbouring scientific fields should be discussed and elucidated. The fields which in this connection are chiefly to be considered are cultural geography, economic history and sociology. If we bear in mind Malinowski's short definition of "functional anthropology" I see no reason why this definition should not apply for Nordic ethnology and more especially for a Nordic ethnology orientated towards the present: "The theory of what human nature is, how human institutions work, what culture does for man at all stages of development." Man at the centre of the study of culture, in other words; and this has in recent years—not only in ethnology—been a constantly repeated slogan.

What significance, then, as a thinking and acting entity has man in our neighbour sciences?

Certainly man is to be found behind the demographic tables, migration-fields, habitation groupings, currents of communication, etc. Ethnogeography aims—and with admirable methods—at a charting of the ant-heap itself, but the individual ant is not in the picture. The human being occurs here always as a collective, as "the mass" in a geographical field of force governed by technics and economy.

There is also what appears to be a promising historical school working with the field of the present, with the main emphasis on community and economic history. There should here be possibilities for a fruitful co-operation with ethnology, especially in the field-work.

As regards Swedish sociology one is, certainly, forced to admit that we have brought to this country only scattered fragments of this science, to which elsewhere, chiefly in America, such importance is attached. In America, as we know, sociology is ranked practically with cultural anthropology. The latter, however, has for a long time been one-sidedly directed towards exotic cultures. But "rural sociology", with its "community studies", has much in common with our occidental ethnology when it is at its best. In Swedish sociology the problems which have hitherto been first on the agenda have been those having to do with contentment and adjustment in a rapidly changing milieu, and there have been many attempts to clarify these problems through public opinion surveys of an often very elementary nature.

The cultural milieu, which despite all rapid changes is none the less always stamped by tradition, has rather consistently failed to engage the interest of the sociologists, which has naturally implied a serious handicap in the work. Nor, indeed, is it easy without a knowledge of the culture-patterns hitherto applying to get a correct notion of the present—even with a from the statistical point of view overwhelming mass of material. Such knowledge is what the ethnologists possess, and this should make it a good deal easier for them to understand the present in all its variety, for it is the business of ethnology to clarify the whole interplay of factors in the culture-milieu, not merely to pick out certain phenomena or complexes of phenomena.

A feature that is common to these three neighbour sciences of ethnology is that none of them is devoted to the study of the actual cultural artefacts in the human milieu, their form, technical development and function—though they do to a certain extent study the economic roles of these artefacts in the geographic field of dissemination and in the temporal transformation. This documentation of the cultural transformation through objects and their continuing roles in rapidly changing culture-milieus is a task for which only ethnologists and museum officials are responsible. This is naturally *in et per se* a strength, because it is such an important cultural task. But it is, as I have already indicated, an enormous work, this matter of documenting in a responsible way both our older culture and its progressive transformation, with its very comprehensive, often difficultly accessible stock of objects, a documentation which in principle must be made with original objects, when this is not possible in models, and always with sufficient illustration by text and pictures. Even if this stock of objects is still only in part collected—and this applies especially to the latest epoch—the museums and other institutions engaged in field-work have nevertheless collected an enormous material, whose classification has really only just begun.

Even if, also in the picture, it will be of interest to elucidate the derivation or distribution of individual culture-elements or culture-complexes—and the possibility of arriving at meaningful results is connected with the possibility of a comparative study extended far beyond our frontiers—even, I say, if such a programme will still have its validity, yet the widened end in view implies first and foremost the demand for studies of man in his milieu.

Since we know, moreover, that the human milieus, not least in our country, vary greatly in time and space, and likewise that especially in the last hundred years or for a somewhat longer period they have been subject to very rapid and very radical transformations, we are led to a research programme that in the first place makes a selection of a series of representative culture-milieus and in the second place finds a method for carrying out depth investigations of these milieus which may afford possibilities of directly comparable and therewith meaningful results.

In the choice of such culture-milieus as objects for research the scope will always depend, of course, on the economic resources of the investigations. In the first place attention should be directed to regions in which relatively extensive field-studies of a more general kind have already been carried out, in which connection one ought also, of course, to consider the documentation through objects. In addition to this, it is obvious that local milieu investigations of an older stratum that have already been begun should be concluded and complemented with comparative investigations in the present. In this way diachronous cross-sections of a certain milieu can relatively soon be obtained, with the consequent possibility of elucidating the culture-transformation. In the Nordic Museum's sphere of activity there are several such imvestigations which have been begun and which for various reasons it has not been possible to carry to a conclusion.

For a definitive assessment of necessary, supplementary, new milieu investigations considerations of many kinds are required. Some of these include giving consideration from the economic-geographic point of view to very varying regions in our country and to the current restructuralization of industrial and economic life, the relation between town and country, densely built-up and thinly populated areas, the relation of the agrarian community to the industrial community, the transformation of the industrial milieus, milieus that have been especially transformed through the changes in the system of communications, regions especially affected by the summer visitors and tourism, etc.

In all these investigations in the field documentation through objects must of course go hand in hand with other modes of documentation.

I should now like to pass on to the problems in the more restricted sense methodical. One is here impelled to put the question: Can we attain to a common method of documentation, a common pattern of model which can make the results comparable even if they are, as is of course inevitable, arrived at by different institutions and different research groups?

It seems that the investigation of a culture-milieu may be made along three different lines or from three aspects: viz. (1). the structure of the culture-milieu; (2) its dynamism, function or activity; and (3) the transformation of the culture-milieu.

In a scientific terminology the concepts ought preferably not to be susceptible of more than one interpretation, and it may therefore be as well to define more closely the terms structure, function and transformation.

Radcliffe-Brown, who has devoted special interest to the concept "social structure", is in 1952 still unclear when he speaks, firstly, of "the structural form, which remains relatively constant" and, secondly, of "the actual social structure, which changes" (1952, p. 192). Here, at one and the same time, a static and a dynamic character are given to the concept "structure". One can, however, accept such definitions as "all social relations of person to person" and "the differentiation of individuals and of classes by their social role" (1952, p. 191). When Radcliffe-Brown speaks of "Social morphology", Social physiology" and "Social change" these concepts also in the main cover what is here meant by structure, function and change. In *Årets äring* (1947, p. 47) I have tried to give a structural classification of the categories of popular tradition. And I have tried to coordinate this structural classification with the structure of the bearers of the tradition themselves, i.e. the human individuals in their groupings and roles (1947, pp. 69 ff; cf. 1964, p. 84).

A structural system of another kind has, as we know, been elaborated by Kurt Lewin in his *Field Theory* (1951). This implies in the main a transference of the field-concepts of gestaltpsychology to the social phenomena. Lewin's field theory still finds an application in culture-geography, and may certainly in many cases also be of value for regional milieu-investigations. It is well adapted for giving an account in schematic form of otherwise difficultly understandable nexuses. However, for an elucidation of the causes and motive forces behind the nexuses it is probably necessary to apply also other analytical models.

In American cultural anthropology various attempts have been made to characterize a certain regional culture by bringing together different characteristics to form a total pattern. Best known are perhaps Ruth Benedict's popularly written works (*Patterns of Culture*, 1934, *The Crysanthemum and the Sword*, 1947). Kroeber has developed this concept somewhat further. He divides "Culture patterns" into four different types (cited here after Hultcrantz 1960): (1) "The functional pattern" (= the culture-elements which exist in all cultures); (2) "The systematic pattern" (= a system or a culture-complex that has proved able to function as an independent entity [in a wider culture-milieu]; (3) "The total culture pattern or basic pattern" (which is fundamental for a certain, whole culture); (4) "The style pattern" (= a limited pattern, which serves as a norm for the carrying out of a certain task or for a certain kind of institution). The type of culture-pattern which is relevant for milieu investigations within a certain culture such as the nordic culture is, of course, rather Kroeber's third type, "the total culture pattern". How such a pattern is to be organized for this purpose is, however, a question which demands special considerations.

Robert Redfield has also worked along this culture-pattern line and in this context has formulated different collective concepts for culture-milieus which are characterized by different kinds of pattern. Such a concept is "Folk Society", which Redfield has placed roughly in opposition to "Urban Society", and he has in a series of papers given a closer analysis of culture-milieus which he considers may be designated as "Folk Societies" (1947, 1950, 1953, 1955, 1956). By "Folk Society" Redfield means the independent primary community almost entirely free of a wider milieu or outside administration, which of course long existed in the part of the world untouched by Western civilization. But the wider geographic contacts and the increasingly developed administrative dependences all over the world naturally make this concept more and more of an ideal concept without many counterparts in reality. For the community in the countryside that is more dependent on the surrounding world Redfield has formulated the concept "Peasant Society" (1956).

Redfield has tried to define these different kinds of culture-milieus (Folk Society, Peasant Society, Urban Society) more closely by ascribing different characteristics to them. In this connection he is moving on the whole within the "Culture pattern" trend. His first definition refers to "The Folk Society" (1947). I have elsewhere commented upon Redfield's seventeen "characteristics" defining "The Folk Society" and at the same time posed the question as to whether this series could be made the basis also for a defining of communities that have been entirely formed by modern West European civilization (1954, pp. 55 f.). In this connection I have also touched upon Oscar Waldemar Junec's study "What is the total pattern of our western civilizations? Some preliminary observations" (1946) and put the question as to whether this system, combined with Redfield's, might serve as a model for comparative milieu-studies in general. Junec has organized his system of "patterns" in another way than Redfield. He groups sixteen different "complexes" or "mainstays" in four main groups and adds to these five definitions which he calls "characteristic complexes of Doctrine and Ethos". Since the systems are different, their parts are not directly comparable; but it is easy to see that Junec's details in the content of the pattern are in practically every point opposed to the details in Redfield's pattern. And this is not so remarkable, as Redfield has on the whole built up his series of "characteristics" as a reverse pattern to our modern civilization.

Both Redfield's pattern for "The Folk Society" and Junec's for "The Western Civilization" really constitute structural, morphological systems but with "in-baked" views of the functional aspect, of the culture-dynamics and also of the culture-change. As far as I can see one would gain increased clarity in the investigation of a culture-milieu if the three above-mentioned aspects, the structure, the function or the dynamics and the change are kept separate in the model at the same time as the same model is to afford the possibility of reciprocal illumination.

I have found that Bronislav Malinowski has set up such a usable model, which by being organized more in detail and with application of Malinowski's analytical reasoning proceeding from the model gives a good picture of the structure of a culture-milieu, its dynamics or function and finally also its transformation and the interacting causes of this transformation. I have also in another connection tested this model of Malinowski's and his analytical reasoning against a material of quite a different kind than Malinowski's, viz. the traditional Swedish peasant milieu, and have found Malinowski's methodical views very useful (1964).

It is naturally unnecessary in this connection to present Malinowski, but to throw my own application of Malinowski's viewpoints into better relief I will give a brief account of the basic notions in his methology. These are, of course, based on a clear scientific foundation and on the understanding of "the human animal". It is only slowly that the community and the institutions are built up which we in our time can make the object for humanistic studies. Man is thus himself the creator of this culture. He lives now in milieus of very different kinds and appears and acts in these milieus in accordance with certain organized systems. Within the systems of these culture-milieus one can purely theoretically distinguish certain groups or categories of completely different kinds. Malinowski calls them "The Concrete Isolates of Organized Behaviour". Within these one can distinguish four categories: charter (attitude to life), personnel (the human individuals in their groupings), norms (rules, knowledge) and material apparatus (the material technical culture-inventory) to which one may in the first place apply a static structural view. These four categories build up, in other words, the culture-structure, the cultural morphology. With the driving forces or catalyzers constituted by human biological needs there is evolved from this richly interwoven structure a cultural activity, a life-form which leads to purposive results, which also as a rule lead to the ever richer, increasingly complicated design of the culture-forms.

These driving forces in the cultural activity are divided up by Malinowski into "Basic needs" and "Derived needs" (i.e. needs appearing in the later cultural development). Whether one proceeds from the human being as individual or as group-being one finds "Cultural responses" (counterparts in the culture-milieu, e.g. the technics and organization of industrial and economic life) corresponding to these basic needs (primary needs, e.g. the need for food) and for their satisfaction.

Taking man's needs as a biological being as his point of departure, Malinowski gives an account of a number of purely physiological impulses which trigger actions resulting in the satisfaction of the individual biological needs. He lists eleven such chains of reaction and stresses that these permanent physiological sequences exist in all cultures, since they belong to man in his quality of biological being (1944, pp. 75 ff.). It is essential for ethnology in its traditional historico-humanistic attitude to take this indisputable biologic foundation into consideration. But once it has been acknowledged, it need not complicate a methodical model built up on Malinowski's trains of thought.

What Malinowski understands as basic needs he has, as we know, divided up into seven groups and has indicated the corresponding projections in the human culture-milieu (cultural responses). These, taken together, constitute the primary grouped community, which can guarantee the lives of its members and the continuing existence of the community.

While these primary needs and their institutional forms in the culture-milieu can guarantee the existence of the primary, let us by all means say primitive, community, there occur in the course of cultural development also what Malinowski calls "Derived needs", based upon man's constant and chronic exploitation of his surrounding for his own good. This leads to a successive organization and institutionalization of the community. The culture-determinism which is a consequence of this becomes in itself as determining as the purely biological determinism.

These new, derived needs, which constantly make themselves felt in a highly developed culture, have also their organizational and institutional counterparts. Malinowski lists them in four groups, and it emerges quite clearly from them which derived needs or "imperatives" they represent: (1) "Economics"; (2) "Social control; (3) "Education"; (4) "Political organization".

Malinowski's trains of thought are often rather intricate, sometimes also contradictory. It would also seem as if, although he had himself revised his manuscript before his decease, Malinowski had not definitively finished the formulation of his trains of thought. But even if his terminology is not always unambiguous or definitively chosen, he reverts so often to the same trains of thought from different points of departure that his conception is quite clear. Without here being in a position to give a detailed account of his different schemata or analytical trains of thought, I have tried to make a simplified model which, when the different elements have been further defined, might serve as a common model both for fieldwork and the documentation of different culture—milieus, and for their understanding and interpretation—in other words, for the elucidation of both structure and function or activity in a culture-milieu and also of its permutations on the temporal plane. Still more simply expressed, it implies elucidating happenings in which driving forces and values of many kinds affect and are affected by a very multi-faceted cultural structure.

With some simplification and some change of Malinowski's schemata and trains of thought and with relatively close reference to the analyses of the structure and function of the popular tradition I gave in *Årets äring* (1947), I have constructed the following model for the study of a culture-milieu—a model which has in any case aimed at general validity as Malinowski did. I do this, like Malinowski, with the help of a diagram (see opposite page).

I have taken the diagram of the culture-structure from Malinowski but with arrows in both directions I have wanted to indicate a reciprocal dependence between the groups.

The four different elements or the groups in this diagram must, of course, be more closely defined and also organized in their details. This is not a matter of any great difficulty. Malinowski has ordered the grouping tendencies and their corresponding institutions in seven groups (1944, pp. 62 ff.). I myself have in another connection distinguished between primary and secondary groupings (1961, pp. 153 ff.), and here it is, of course, possible to choose different divisions. The same is the case with the division of the large group formed by the culture-inventory. A division must here naturally be made according to function and not according to form.

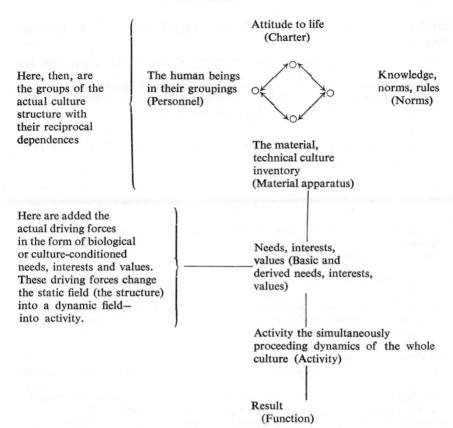

Here, then, are the groups of the actual culture structure with their reciprocal dependences

The human beings in their groupings (Personnel)

Attitude to life (Charter)

Knowledge, norms, rules (Norms)

The material, technical culture inventory (Material apparatus)

Here are added the actual driving forces in the form of biological or culture-conditioned needs, interests and values. These driving forces change the static field (the structure) into a dynamic field— into activity.

Needs, interests, values (Basic and derived needs, interests, values)

Activity the simultaneously proceeding dynamics of the whole culture (Activity)

Result (Function)

The actual activity in the culture-milieu is, of course, elucidated in space, time and with reference to the social relations. With regard to the space-aspect such schemata as Kurt Lewin's field may be very useful. With respect to the actual time factor within the cultural dynamics the actual major cycles must, of course, be incorporated in the system (the ages of human life, certain administrative periods, the division of the business year and the calendar year, the hours of the day and night). Especially, in this connection, must the internal rhythm of these time-divisions, and therewith their varying stress on need, interest and value be carefully considered. I have dealt with these questions in a relatively great deal in *Årets äring* (1944, pp. 40 ff.).

Finally, I will point out that I have replaced Malinowski's concept "function" as a designation for the result of the cultural activity, with the more neutral word result. Another word that would fit here might be "goal". The reason for this is that Malinowski has used the concept "function" in rather various senses and never, actually, fixed his definite understanding.

In order, in conclusion, to say something of the need to study also the change of the culture-milieus, I am of the opinion that a properly elaborated model for the study of the culture-milieu—thus not necessarily the one here presented—will permit of comparable cross-sections at different dates and for different stages of development of a culture-milieu—perhaps not least in the field of the present—to give us meaningful comparisons with older conditions.

REFERENCES

ESKERÖD, ALBERT (1947) Årets äring, Lund. (Summary in English).

ESKERÖD, ALBERT (1953–4) Folk society and Western civilization, in *Folkliv*, pp. 53–61.

ESKERÖD, ALBERT (1961) Soziale organization in *Schwedische Volkskunde*, pp. 153–79, Uppsala.

ESKERÖD, ALBERT (1964) Needs, interests, values and the supernatural, in *Studia Ethnographica Upsaliensia*, Vol. 21, pp. 81–98, Lund.

HULTCRANTZ, ÅKE (1960) *General Ethnological Concepts*, Copenhagen.

JUNEC, OSCAR WALDEMAR (1946) What is the total pattern of our Western civilizations? Some preliminary observations, in *American Anthropologist*, pp. 397–406.

LEWIN, KURT (1951) *Field Theory in Social Science*, New York.

MALINOWSKI, BRONISLAV (1930) Anthropology and administration, in *Africa*, pp. 428 f.

MALINOWSKI, BRONISLAV (1944) *A Scientific Theory of Culture and Other Essays*, Chapel Hill.

RADCLIFFE-BROWN, A. R. (1923) The methods of ethnology and Social anthropology, in *South African Ass. for Advancement of Science*, Vol. 21, pp. 124–47.

REDFIELD, ROBERT (1947) The Folk Society, in *The American Journal of Sociology*, Vol. 52, No. 4, pp. 293–308 A.

REDFIELD, ROBERT (1950) *A Village that Chose Progress*, Chicago.

REDFIELD, ROBERT (1953) *The Primitive World and its Transformation*, Ithaca.

REDFIELD, ROBERT (1955) *The Little Community*, 1st ed., Uppsala.[1]

REDFIELD, ROBERT (1956) *Peasant Society and Culture*, Chicago.[1]

[1] Edited together in Phoenix Books, Chicago, 1961.

ETHNOLOGICAL RESEARCH ON THE PRESENT IN FINLAND: SOME PROBLEMS AND ASPECTS

ILMAR TALVE

Institute of Ethnology, University of Turku

THE MODERN ERA AND THE PRESENT

This symposium has been devoted to "anthropological research on the present" and in the invitation the terms "the modern era" and "the present" are used as synonyms. This has led me at the beginning of this lecture to touch briefly upon these terms, as the question of what anthropological research on the present is to be, and not be, is in a high degree dependent upon the import to be given to them. In Nordic ethnology the terms "the modern era" or "present epoch" are current expressions and have been used in different works to designate the time that is within living memory, from which time we can thus get material which both quantitatively and qualitatively can form a satisfactory basis for an ethnological analysis. The older now living generation, those 60 and 70 years old and still older, can give from their own recollections information about the conditions prevailing around the turn of the century, or, rather, about the period between the turn of the century and the First World War. This period would thus form the lower time-limit for "the modern era", the upper time-limit is our own time, "the present".[1]

Since the ethnological collecting through questionnaires, etc., in all the Nordic countries is to a certain extent still going on, the modern era has automatically come to occupy the focus of attention, for the simple reason that older material can no longer be collected. On the other hand, at least in Finland, there has not often been a conscious attitude towards a moving of the time-limit nearer to our own time or to the present. Nor, among Finnish ethnologists, has any particular interest been shown in the innovations which only in this period, i.e. since the

---

[1] The term "present epoch" derives from S. Erixon, *Svenskt Folkliv* (1938), p. 286. By the side of this the expression "older present epoch" has also been used to designate the period before "the present epoch", i.e. 1850–1900, the time forming the period for *Atlas of Swedish Folk Culture* and for several ethnological dissertations.

turn of the century, have intruded in folklife. When collecting they have preferred to follow the continuity of nineteenth-century objects into this century. They have also paid more attention to the older features than to the completely new features or to changes occurring during this century. It may thus be said that in Finland "the modern era" has now also made its entry in ethnological research, but this is due to the inevitable forward movement of the times. And researchers have not often drawn the necessary consequences and consciously adapted research and collecting to the present situation. However, a change has already taken place, and also the general view has begun to be changed.

As regards the investigation of phenomena in our own time, in the present, folklife researchers have in general been rather reserved, as it has been considered that for the ethnologist the concept tradition has decisive importance. Concerning an innovation, it cannot immediately be said that it will get any firm anchorage in folklife or not, and whether it will become traditional or not. But this means that ethnologists will take up a wait-and-see position as regards novelties, and the so-called initial stage, to use an expression of Rehnberg's,[2] will go past us without any attention being paid to this stage. The consequence is that research will get under way too late, and although one can get information about this initial stage later, also I think that to take up a-too-rigid standpoint on principle is a disadvantage. Without needing to give up the concept "tradition" in our research, we can in connection with different novelties in our own time (innovations in the present), set to work at once in order to be able to elucidate more closely what is happening in this stage. I think that in this connection research can attain results which can be used also to throw light upon phenomena which have really become traditional, quite irrespective of whether an innovation whose acceptance the researcher is investigating itself becomes traditional or not. As we cannot with certainty decide in advance which innovations will become traditional or not, we must, in order to elucidate the initial stage with its process of acceptance, investigate different phenomena in our own time. Naturally, a wise selection is necessary in this case. If we are lucky, and the phenomenon being investigated becomes traditional, we have elucidated the initial stage in detail. The same investigator or someone else can after a time, for instance after 10 years, take up the same phenomenon for new treatment, and elucidate the following period, when the

[2] M. Rehnberg, *Ljusen på gravarna och andra ljusseder* (1965) *(The Lights on the Graves and Other Lighting Customs)*.

historical dimension will enter and the investigation then becomes tradi-tion-historical.

For the actualization of ethnological research it is therefore necessary to extend it to include also completely new phenomena, chiefly to show how innovations develop in the modern era and what factors one has to reckon with in this connection. I think that in this way we shall get above all methodically valuable results with a more general scope, usable in different contexts. But one also creates in this way a basis for continued research in subsequent years, if the innovations become incorporated in the popular culture, i.e. become traditional.

By the side of this task, also the time remembered by the persons now living must be accounted as belonging to ethnological research on the modern era, and this research must be as all-round as possible. In the first place we must in the next few years, at least in Finland, work at col-lecting the primary material to throw light upon the folk-groups and occupational groups that have been overlooked by the earlier work of collecting.

For the above-mentioned reasons I shall therefore in the following use the term "research on the modern era" for the period from about the turn of the century up to our time, and the term "the present" (or "ethnological research on the present") for investigations of our own times, i.e. the phenomena in the 1960's.

INVESTIGATION OF THE PRESENT IN FINLAND

As my task in this connection is also to give an account of the situation of research in Finland, I will not completely pass over "research in the present" or "innovations in the present", although what I have to say will be rather little, since the ethnologists in Finland have in general not engaged in research on new phenomena in our own time. However, some attempts have been made.

As in my opinion the so-called "initial stage" of innovations is of great interest for ethnological research, irrespective of whether an innovation afterwards becomes traditional or not, we have in Åbo taken some such innovations under observation. Such a problem has arisen in connection with a study of current children's games in Åbo, with Raumo and Salo as towns for comparison, with the main stress on their popularity and the so-called intensity. The material for the study was collected in elementary schools through elementary school teachers who were studying ethnology and taking part in training-college exercises. There were, however, not so many of them that a more comprehensive, simultaneously carried out investigation was possible. But the greater part of the material was collected in the year 1962. In the autumn of the same year a new children's game came to Åbo, a so-called "rubber-band twist", a skipping game played chiefly by the girls. It quickly gained a footing and became very popular, and we were able to observe what a revolution it caused in the "popularity-field", if the term may be allowed to pass, of the girls' games. It was not, however, possible to elucidate in detail the actual initial stage, partly because the investigation was started a little too late, unaware as we were of what was happening in the world of children's games, and partly, as usual, owing to shortage of workers. I can only add that this game has become traditional, and still enjoys great popularity. For the rest, the result of the investigation showed that the most popular games in all three towns studied were the old games known already in the 1920's and still earlier.[3] This investigation thus has to do with urban culture.

Another innovation that is just now becoming increasingly general in Åbo is the custom of tying little wreaths to the outer door of apartments at Christmas. As we had no possibilities to follow the spreading of this custom in detail in the whole city, we chose one quarter where it was recorded at Christmas 1966. Since all sent in their census-returns to the police at the turn of the year, we intend later to interview the persons in question and ascertain the factors that contributed to their acceptance of this innovation. In Sweden it is considerably older. Comparative random samples have been taken in other quarters of the city.

THE MOST IMPORTANT ELEMENT IN RESEARCH ON THE PRESENT FROM THE FINNISH POINT OF VIEW

In Finland the earlier ethnological collecting activity up to the 1950's was almost exclusively focused on the countryside, on the peasant culture. But the unpropertied class of the country districts—artisans, fishermen, crofters, servants, farm-hands of the poorest class—have been sufficiently taken into consideration, as these social groups were to a great extent passed over by earlier research. The culture of the country districts was understood solely as a peasant culture, and, moreover, as a peasant culture with a uniform stamp throughout. The deficiencies in the earlier collecting activity become all the more evident because the old peasant

---

[3] Cf. I. Talve, Turun, Rauman ja Salon nykyisistä lastenleikeistä (On the present-day children's games in Åbo, Raumo and Salo), *Kalevalaseuran Vuosikirja* **47**, 1967.

culture itself began to disintegrate in the latter half of the nineteenth century on account of industrialization and other causes, which on the whole have been similar in all the Nordic countries. This development, as we know, provided the subject of the Nordic meeting of folklife researchers that was held in the year 1959 in Åbo, where "the disintegration of the old peasant culture" was discussed.

This is why in Finland we have now been confronted with two great, very comprehensive and even urgent tasks. On the one hand we lack the material to throw light on the culture-milieu and living conditions of the new class, the workers, whose number in the last decades of the nineteenth century and up to the First World War increased very rapidly. This coincides in part with the simultaneous growth of the urban population and the advent of new densely built-up areas in the countryside. But the urban culture is not only a worker-culture, and the urban culture therefore forms a separate sector in the collecting activity.

On the other hand, material relating to the countryside must also be collected, partly to throw light on the stage of disintegration or rather transformation of the peasant culture and the culture of the country districts, partly also to give a proper perspective and right background to investigations relating to worker and urban culture during the same period.[4] It is necessary to aim at a total view. One must not depreciate the loyalty to tradition of the worker and urban culture in comparison with the peasant culture from a completely different period, e.g. the first part of the nineteenth century, comparisons should be drawn with the contemporary culture of the country districts.

The difficulties encountered in carrying out these tasks have been the usual ones, that is, shortage of personnel and money. To these must be added difficulties of another kind. In Finland the old traditional view of ethnology as a discipline dealing with the old peasant culture and carrying on pure research on objects under historical aspects has been firmly rooted and still is so among the general public. Since according to this view the country districts, under the influence of industrialism and the new classes, did not represent the old order and thus did not either have any proper traditional culture, it is considered that the whole problem really falls outside ethnology's field of work. If one asks who are to occupy themselves with this period and the new social groups one seldom gets satisfactory answers. It is only in recent years that this view of the position and tasks

[4] See further I. Talve, Kansatiede ja murroskausi (Ethnology and the period of transition), *Suomalainen Suomi*, 1958, pp. 432–40, and I. Talve, Suomalainen kansatiede (Finnish ethnology), *Scripta ethnologica* 14, Åbo, 1963, pp. 24 ff.

of ethnology has gradually begun to break down, but it still constitutes a considerable hindrance when one is to present and motivate one's investigation projects and get grants to carry them out. On the other hand, in the Finnish labour movement, where a certain interest in worker culture has been aroused, the requirements of the situation have been all too narrowly and dogmatically understood, and the political aspects and those having to do with the history of the trade unions have been favoured at the expense of the general ethno-historical aspects. Grants have been made for the collection of memories from the breakthrough years of the labour and trade-union movement, but the attitude to the further investigations aiming to throw light upon the workers' living milieus and the general culture conditions has been negative.[5]

(a) *Worker and occupational culture*

The collections of material to throw light upon the worker culture and the different occupations were started in Åbo in the year 1958, A more detailed account of these endeavours is probably unnecessary in this context. So far it has been possible to procure material concerning lumberjacks, log-floaters, sawmill workers, railway workers and navvies, seamen, countryside artisans and concerning servants in the country districts. A questionnaire relating to building workers is being distributed.[6] The first stage in each one of the investigations has been to draw up and distribute a list of questions in the subject. This is the cheapest and therefore actually the only practicable way in which we can make an investigation. The material from our informants has then as a rule been complemented with interviews and field-work inventories to the extent to which the material resources have been available. Thanks to the fact that Åbo University received from the Wihuri fund, in the year 1965, a sizable donation in support of so-called "bigger humanistic investigation

[5] Cf. J. Eenilä, Suomalainen työväenkulttuurin tutkimus ja sen merkitys (Investigation of the Finnish worker culture and its importance) *Suomen Sosiaalidemokraatti*, no. 34, 5/2, 1967.

[6] Cf. further I. Talve, *Arbeit und Lebensverhältnisse der finnischen Bahnbauarbeiter und Eisenbahner*, Åbo, 1964, pp. 6 ff. Some smaller studies, based on the collected material, have been published; cf. for example, I. Talve, *Satakunnan uittotyöläisistä* (Summary in translation: *Die Flösser in Satakunta*), 1961; I. Talve, *Suomen sahatyöläisten työstä, työajasta ja palkkaustavasta ennen 1920-lukua* (Summary: *On the Work, Working Hours, and Wages of Sawmill Workers in Finland before 1920*), 1962; J. Eenilä, *Uitto ja uittotyöläiset Paimionjoen vesistössä* (Summary in translation: *Die Flösserei und die Flösser im Gewässer des Flusses Paimionjoki*), 1965—all in the series *Scripta ethnologica*. The lumberjacks in Finland have been dealt with in a thesis for licentiate by Jukka Eenilä.

projects", the Ethnological Institution has now in the years 1966 and 1967 also got money to carry on collecting activity more systematically during a 5-year period, 1966–70.

The second possibility has been to use the students as personnel in connection with the inventories, and it has subsequently been possible to use the interview material collected by them in training college work. In this way quite a large number of local investigations have been carried out in the 1960's, although on a small scale; but these may form necessary points of departure for more detailed inventories in the future. The following factory settlements have been investigated in this way: Littois (clothes factory);[7] Tervakoski, Äänekoski and Mänttä (paper and pulp industries); Iittala, Riihimäki, Karhula (glass industry), Dalsbruk (ironworks), Korkeakoski (shoe factory).

In this connection one may also pose a question that must be borne in mind by all who are engaged in the collection of memories—just how reliable is the material one gets together in this way? Naturally, where investigations of occupations and industrial settlements are carried on systematically, for example with a view to publication in monograph form, ethnological research must make use of archives and other available sources for control and supplementation. But the reliability of the recollections collected is nevertheless the central source-critical problem. The reliability of the workers' recollections in North Sweden has recently been subjected to a control by the historian Bo Gustafsson in his study on the Norrland sawmill workers.[8] In this connection he arrives at, from our point of view, a very encouraging result, as he considers the source-value of the workers' recollections to be rather high also where they are a matter of statements concerning working hours, wages and housing conditions. This should further stimulate the collection of recollections and the using of these as sources for ethnological research.

The collecting of material to throw light upon the workers' milieu and living conditions during the breakthrough of industrialism has in general been so much delayed, also as regards industrialization in Finland, that we cannot now find material throwing light upon the first stage. Only in exceptional cases can such material be gained. Second-hand information (e.g. the children's stories about their parents) is another source,

[7] Cf. H. Saarikivi, *Littoisten verkatehtaan työoloista vv. 1880–1920* (Summary in translation: *Über die Arbeitsverhältnisse an der Tuchfabrik in Littoinen 1880–1920*), *Scripta ethnologica*, 13, Åbo, 1963.

[8] Bo Gustafsson, *Den norrländska sågverksindustrins arbetare 1890–1913*, Uppsala, 1965, pp. 208 ff.

but the amount is in any case slight. The chief material throwing light upon this period must therefore be procured from other sources. However, we can console ourselves with one thing: in the majority of worker occupations in Finland the really significant changes in operation (this might also be called "the second mechanization stage") did not take place until the 1920's or even later. The First World War enters here as a delaying factor. One consequence of this has been that the worker milieu from and including the breakthrough of industrialism up to the 1920's has been comparatively stable. The changes have not been so great during this period. Conditions are naturally a little different in different occupations and different industries. Thanks to this, however, we can, if we can get reliable material from the period around the turn of the century, with the help of this material indirectly throw light on the whole stage. The possibilities of doing this must naturally be weighed from case to case and under strict source-critical aspects.

(b) *Urban Culture*

The towns as a rule possess in their archives very comprehensive series of filed material which forms a good basis also for urban-ethnological research. In Åbo it is this material, chiefly estate inventories, that have been used, for the time being for some training-college essays. But the archive material needs to be supplemented for the picture to be as all-round as possible. In connection with certain aspects of folk-culture in the towns, however, interview material and answers to questionnaires constitute the only possible solution.

Some valuable works on folklife in the towns have already earlier been published in Finland, but these are few in number. As one of the earlier "urban ethnologists" in the whole of Europe one may mention the great collector Samuli Paulaharju, since as early as the year 1925 he published a stimulating book on folklife in "Vanha Raahe" (Old Brahestad).[9]

However, the collecting of ethnological material in the towns was started late in Finland, later than among the workers, this was on account of shortage of personnel. In Åbo we were able in the year 1966 to produce a first questionnaire for Åbo and Gammelkarleby in central Österbotten. This material is to be supplemented with interviews. In Åbo this has been done already earlier through students and to a larger extent through scholarship-holders in the year 1966. During this year interviews

---

[9] Cf. further I. Talve, Kansatiede kaupungissa (Ethnological urban research), *Suomalainen Suomi*, 1961, pp. 11–17.

are to be started also in Björneborg. To some extent, too,   certain special lists of questions concerning urban culture have been studied, such as the above-mentioned investigation of the children's games (cf. note 3), customs in connection with annual festivals,[10] doorwreaths for Christmas, schoolchildren's customs and certain groups of artisans in the town (in Åbo, for instance, coppersmiths,[11] tailors, seamstresses, etc.). To begin with, students have been used for such studies, and they have written training-college essays on the subject. As source-material have been used interviews, newspapers and published recollections, to a certain extent also archive material. These are to be regarded as preliminary studies for a first survey, and they were followed with the drawing up of more detailed lists of questions.

In connection with ethnological invsstigations in towns the problem of the delimitation of the area necessarily arises, unless investigations are being carried on in a very small town of 1000–2000 inhabitants. The town is seldom a uniform ecological region. The different parts of the town, even the quarters, have their own history and date of appearance, and the structure of the population is very heterogeneous. In this situation it seems scarcely possible to try to investigate the whole town all at one time, except in the collecting stage with the thematic questionnaires. In Finland, at least, the personnel and economic resources are insufficient for so large scale investigations. Therefore we have tried to start local, delimited depth-studies in the different quarters of the city. The task then becomes easier on account of the structure and origin of the population. Such an investigation is under way in Beckholmen, situated in the harbour area, and another is projected in a part of the city in which the houses have been built by the workers' housing associations. The same sort of delimitation of the area has been applied also elsewhere in Scandinavia, e.g. in Copenhagen and in Lund.

If in connection with urban culture one gets onto the question of its relation to the surrounding countryside,[12] the problem is difficult to master

[10] Cf. for example, Lasse Laaksonen, *Turkulaisten julkisia vappuperinteitä vuosina 1919–1960* (Summary in translation: *Das öffentliches Feiern des 1. Mai in Turku von 1919 bis 1960*), *Scripta ethnologica 15*, Åbo, 1963.

[11] Cf. L. Ranne, *Eräs turkulainen vaskisepänverstas* (Summary in translation: *Eine Kupferschiede in Turku*). *Scripta ethnologica 9*, Åbo, 1961. A longer work by the same author on the coppersmiths in Åbo (219 pages) was presented as a graduate paper in the year 1966.

[12] Also S. Svensson, in a review of H. Commenda, *Volkskunde der Stadt Linz I–II in Rig 1961*, p. 129, has pointed out that one of the chief questions for coming urban studies must be the relation between town and surrounding countryside.

if the town investigated is large. Also for this reason those parts of a town in which the demographic structure is fairly uniform may be suitable points of departure in the first stage. In Finland it has already earlier been observed that the population in certain small towns comes to a great extent from the immediate vicinity, from the parishes around the town.[13] In such cases the problem is a good deal easier to investigate: the town and the countryside do not form sharp contrasts but are from the ethnological point of view rather two sides of the same coin. The comparisons then become easier and the researcher can survey the whole area the whole time. The total view must also in the urban investigations be an important guiding principle.

(c) *The Countryside after "the disintegration of the old peasant culture"*

The folklife in the country districts during the critical period in which removals and emigration took away a lot of people, especially among the unpropertied and the younger generation, is on the whole as yet uninvestigated. Since the ethnological collecting activity has been focused on the people in the country districts, however, valuable information has been collected, although not systematically. This material is unfortunately widely scattered and mixed up with other material, and can only with great trouble be searched out.

It has in Finland therefore been necessary, as mentioned in the foregoing, to start a new collection to throw light upon folklife in the country districts in the transitional period. It has been possible to begin this only with the help of questionnaires, and the aim of the collecting has chiefly been to record and date the changes in different sectors of folklife. The lists of questions have been thematic and the aim has been to procure new material for the researchers which should give them the possibility of starting more detailed, thematic or locally restricted investigations. Questionnaires have been distributed from Åbo on subjects like the changes in popular customs (baptisms, weddings, burials), the division of labour between men and women, the changes in diet, the upbringing of children and family life, the mechanization of agriculture and the reorganization of hunting teams to newer hunting groups.[13a]

The change of folk-culture in the country districts cannot, however, be illustrated only with thematic surveys, even if these are really detailed investigations. The most important social factor of the country districts

[13] Cf. M. Klöverkorn, *Die sprachliche Struktur Finnlands 1880–1950*, Helsingfors, 1960, pp. 228 ff.

[13a] Cf. now V. Anttila, Die Elchjagdgenossenschaften in Finnland im Herbst, 1966 Scripta ethnologica, 24. Turku, 1968.

has been the old village. It therefore seems to be necessary to organize also local depth-studies by the side of thematic investigations on larger areas (parishes, provinces or the whole country). These local investigations of communities can give us concrete examples of what really happened during this period in the villages, what changes were the most important and for what reason. In western Finland, which is an old region for village culture, I have been able to observe, in connection with some village studies, that the villages nowadays have on the whole just as large settlement and population, though divided up in a different way, as at the end of the seventeenth century. But they had quite a different appearance and had a much bigger population especially in the nineteenth century when the numbers of the unpropertied classes culminated.[14] At the end of the nineteenth century really great changes took place in the villages in connection with industrialization and the removals. Light can be thrown upon these only through local investigations. The old method of village-studies seems to be worth taking up again, perhaps as an inter-Nordic research project. These studies must nowadays be planned thematically in another way, be extended—and preferably be carried out as team-work in collaboration with sociologists and historians. Light must then be thrown on the village in all its aspects and the development charted during a century, about 1865–1965.

Some such new village-studies have been planned in Åbo, but not yet carried out. In order to be in a position to get a really historical dimension it will be necessary, to begin with, to choose a village where one has already earlier, in the 1920's, collected material that can now no longer be collected.[15] A village-study carried out as team-work is an expensive investigation, and for this reason alone the object must be chosen with care to attain good results.

As in Sweden, smaller municipalities in Finland are nowadays being amalgamated to form larger units, big municipalities, and neighbouring municipalities are incorporated with these. Certain rural districts in the vicinity of the towns, in which the ecological and demographic structure has been radically changed in the last hundred years, but

[14] Cf. for example, I. Talve, *Lemlahden kylä* (Summary in translation: *Das Dorf Lemlahti in Satakunda*), *Scripta ethnologica* 6, Åbo, 1960, and I. Talve, *Huomioita kylien muuttumisesta Paattisten pitäjän pohjoisosassa* (Summary in translation: *Über die Veränderung der Dörfer im nördlichen Teil des Ksp Paattinen, Eigentliches Finnland*), *Scripta ethnologica* **8**, Åbo, 1961.

[15] In Åbo a study of a coastal village in Pyhämaa parish in Finland proper has been projected. The village was investigated for the first time (chiefly the village plan and buildings) in the year 1928.

where the old sector (the peasant population and the agriculture) is still partly preserved, seem also to be especially suitable for the ethnologist to be able to chart in detail "the great transformation". In Åbo we have chosen a neighbour municipality to Åbo, Reso, whose municipal administration has shown great interest and also given financial support. An investigation that was started there a couple of years ago is to study the folklife and folk-culture in Reso during a century, about 1860–1960, from all the more important aspects.

An important group in the country districts was formerly constituted by the different artisans. Handicrafts in the countryside are now dying out completely, or are just now undergoing such great changes that the result is practically the same. It thus seems an urgent task to collect material about artisans now, while it is still possible. In this connection attention must be paid not only to changes in the structure and techniques of the occupation, but also, and above all, to the artisans as a social group. With the support of the State Humanistic Commission such investigations have been carried on for several years (1962–65) in Finland proper from Åbo. In the year 1962 information was collected from the municipalities concerning all the artisans now active (and also older ones). In the province their number was about 250. A large number, almost 20 per cent, chiefly the older ones, have already died. Of those remaining, about 200, it has been possible to interview about 170. The chief aim of the investigation has been to chart the country handicraftsmen's living conditions, where they served their apprenticeship, their clientèle, working techniques and so forth, before and around the turn of the century, and later up to our own times. Other sources will of course be utilized besides the interview material. Apart from getting a picture in this way of the artisans during the period which followed the introduction of the freedom of trade (in Finland in the years 1868, 1869), we have also got material that permits comparisons between the worker and urban culture during the same period.

SOME PROBLEMS OF METHOD

(a) *The Question of Loyalty to Tradition*

One often hears the statement that the new urban and worker cultures are subject to rapid change and that tradition is therefore of little importance for them. The worker and urban culture is considered to be an international standard culture which from the point of view of tradition is not very profitable; instead of folk-culture we have here an international culture. In this connection comparisons are often made with the peasant culture in the country districts, which is considered to be a stable, traditional folk-culture. Here, however, it is often forgotten that two different periods are spoken of. In the worker and urban culture in the breakthrough years of industrialism, and later the actual ecological ground is another. The population is more mobile, the social structure is in process of change, and the changes are continuous. The whole course of development is dynamic. In these circumstances one can scarcely expect tradition to have the same vitality as in a pre-industrial rural milieu. For comparisons, however, we lack investigations from the country districts during the same period. In those cases in which comparisons have been made, on the other hand, one may even question whether the country district is more tradition-bound than the worker and urban culture.

In Finland we have a striking example of the way in which the conditions really developed through an investigation by Paavo Kortekangas, D.D., on the church life in an industrial community, where the conditions in Tammerfors for half a century (1855–1905) are studied.[16] The author was able to establish, *inter alia*, that during the first period of industrialization the working population in Tammerfors was more church-going, more traditional, than the population in the countryside nearest to Tammerfors during the same period. It was only after this that the relation of the working population began slowly to change, and the firm hold of tradition was broken at the commencement of the turn of the century. This example throws light upon only one sector of folklife, but it may nevertheless serve as a warning to those who want without further ado to declare urban and worker culture to be without tradition and peasant culture to be traditional. As yet unfortunately we know all too little about the vitality of the traditions in the country districts "after the disintegration of the old peasant culture".

(b) *The Question of the Old Ethnological Categories*

Those who have followed what in recent years has been written in ethnological literature about the investigation of urban and worker culture will have observed that there is considerable obscurity. Especially in German quarters writers have discussed the question of whether the ethnological concepts or categories in investigations on peasant culture

[16] P. Kortekangas, *Kirkko ja uskonnollinen elämä teollistuvassa yhteiskunnassa. Tutkimus Tampereesta 1855–1905 (Church and the religious life in a community on the way to industrialization. A study on Tammerfors 1855–1905)*, Helsingfors, 1965.

can also be used when one is studying a more recent period or other population groups, or whether we must devise completely new concepts. The problem is closely connected with the question of the goals and means of worker and urban ethnology, but is not quite the same thing.

In investigations on peasant culture one works with group-concepts such as economy, agriculture, cattle-rearing, fishing and so on. One treats in this connection implements, methods and also social aspects. In the same way one studies the building culture, home furnishing, costumes, diet, customs and usages. The basis for peasant culture is formed by the economy, by the ecological system, which are needed for the maintenance of life. Implements and methods are in this connection the tradition-bound factors which give a framework to the whole structure.

In the worker's world, in his work for a livelihood, in his "economy" the central concept is the machine. It cannot be considered to be, nor is it a traditional tool. And on this account the importance of investigating the life of the worker has been depreciated; it is considered that the worker's "economy" is not traditional, not popular, of the people. But in this connection one must take the foundation itself as one's point of departure, the work-process in an occupational group, because the whole existence of the group rests upon this. The worker's position in the work-process, at the machine, is reflected in different ways in his life and milieu: upon this depends not only his and his family's existence, but also his position in his own social group both inside and outside of the factory area. This indirectly affects his family conditions, the family's position in the community, its social status.

The ethnologist who is working on an investigation of worker culture must thus first familiarize himself with the work-process and record the changes occurring during the period dealt with in his study. These as a rule affect the whole occupational group and all its relations. The technical and mechanical development belong naturally to the history of techniques but it must also be taken into account by the ethnologist. So-called rationalization is never solely a technical problem—it causes, as a rule, the changes in the work-process which directly or indirectly affect the worker—the human being and the economic and social structure of the entire occupational group.

The work-process deserves to be taken into consideration also for other reasons. For different tasks in the work-process the worker is confronted with new demands on his competence. Different tasks require different kinds of skills. With this is connected the very interesting question of the training for the job. In former times, when there were no occupational schools and no textbooks, the work in industry was learned in the same way as in the peasant and artisan milieu—through direct instruction by the older man the work-process was learned by the younger men. In the working-class there was in the same way as among peasants and artisans a *work-tradition*, transferred by older bearers of the tradition to the younger untaught novices. The work-tradition also forms the backbone of professional pride. An intricate and difficult to learn work-tradition gave the occupation greater dignity and esteem. The points of contact with the artisan milieu are here rather transparent, It is, however, already now rather difficult in certain occupations to make clear how the propagation of the work-tradition took place; but there are still possibilities of collecting material to throw light on this important question.

Apart from the work-process, the workers' economy includes also the question of wages. Nor is this concept new, it is an important problem in the artisan milieu but also in the country district, e.g. among servants and the unpropertied. Wage developments as such can be followed statistically, but the problem belongs to the economic-historical research-field. The ethnologist should interest himself in wages in so far as he considers this necessary in order to form his own opinion of the living standard of the occupational group. One should have concrete grounds to go on if one is to give an account of the economic possibilities of the occupational group or the worker. If one is to throw light upon "the actual life" in the worker-milieu, then the cash wage and the payments in kind are important grounds, as self-evident as when one investigates the peasant's economy in kind in older epochs as the basis for the group's existence.

In the peasant culture one may speak of the main occupations and side-lines and these concepts can also be used in urban and worker milieu. Frequently, however, the so-called side-lines are reduced to the payments in kind (a piece of land to cultivate), and they acquire in this way also the stamp of a spare-time occupation. There are, however, different occupational groups for which agriculture and cattle rearing are side-lines in the full sense of the word—to these belong most of the workers living scattered about in the country districts (lumberjacks, log-floaters, etc.), but also in the densely built-up areas (certain groups of railwaymen and so on). The dividing line between worker and small farmer is in certain occupations in the country districts rather blurred, in the same way as among artisans and others in the country; but these groups are thereby also interesting intermediate forms of agrarian and industrial living milieu.

The old ethnological concept economy, which is used in investigations of peasant culture, may in my opinion be retained, but must be modified. One may call it "working life" or simply "work". This concept is also in the worker and urban milieu economic sector of the culture, and it exercises a lasting influence on the different institutions in the culture-system.

As regards certain other ethnological basic questions the general remark should be made that in investigating these questions in urban or worker milieu one ought not, in the first place, proceed from the type or form criteria. Instead of form and type, the main stress should be laid upon function and structure.

The form and type criteria have their significance in the peasant culture, since one proceeds on the assumption that on the whole the peasant culture was a uniform culture spread over the whole country. As on the basis of type and form criteria one can elucidate the distribution and the course of development in a large area, these results can be used to form certain ethno-historical conclusions to throw light on the development of the peasant culture. In the worker and urban cultures, on the other hand, which do not cover extensive connected areas with a similar tradition, type and form criteria have not such a central importance. They should not be forgotten, but must be subordinated to other criteria.

I mean, in other words, that when carrying out worker and urban investigations one should not have as one's point of departure certain traditional concepts, as one has in studies of peasant culture; one must take the whole, the ecological structure characterizing the group, as one's starting-point. If, for instance, one is studying the "farming" or potato-cultivation of sawmill workers from the form or type point of view, one may arrive at results which have nothing of interest to offer from the ethnological point of view. The men perhaps do not use ploughs, but employ quite fortuitous implements borrowed from others, or even completely new factory-manufactured tools. In spite of this, the sawmill worker's potato field in his own milieu may be just as traditional a phenomenon as a similar field worked by a countryside crofter or cotter. It may even have more value and economic importance for the sawmill worker and his family than for the others, who till their field allotments with old traditional implements according to traditional methods. The same applies to various other "side-lines" in worker and urban cultures, which appear to be unimportant and nondescript from the type or form point of view but have an important function in the life of the occupational group and form a traditional part in its ecological structure.

In worker and urban studies the ecological structure and the composition of the population (demographic problems) form the point of departure, the basis. The different ethnological categories of folk-culture should in the first place be regarded from the functional point of view. Following Richard Weiss' way of viewing the matter it may be said that instead of buildings one ought to study the living in them instead of the costume the clothes (*Tracht contra Kleidung*), and instead of the different dishes one should investigate what, how and when they are eaten. One thus comes rather close to what Malinowski's functionalism aims at: "to elucidate ethnological facts by considering their function, by considering their significance within the integral system of the culture, by considering the ways in which they are linked to each other within the system and by considering the relation of this system to the physical environment". (Hereafter Nicolaisen, *Primitiva kulturer* (*Primitive Cultures*), p. 145.)

By the side of the working life the above-mentioned three categories, dwelling, clothes and food, belong to what is most essential if one wants to describe the culture milieu and the living conditions in a certain occupational group or, for example, in a certain quarter of a town. The main stress in connection with the dwelling or living thus falls not upon the form criteria (= types of building in the peasant culture), but on the functional—the dwelling, its use and how it is furnished. Instead of the type of building, it is the type of dwelling that in the industrial and urban milieu is what is central and important. The buildings may be built by the employer or by some entrepreneur in the town, and they are naturally influenced by the tendencies of the period and have their own culture-historical background. But they are not folk-traditional in the sense in which the building types of the countryside are. The folk-traditional element in the worker and urban milieu, on the other hand, appears in the dwelling itself in connection with its use and furnishing. This is where ethnological research has its central task. Workers' recollections and interviews constitute reliable material for these questions: it is almost the rule that in his old age a person can describe his childhood home in detail.

If, on the other hand, one wants to get some idea of the housing standard among workers or, for example, the poorer classes in a town, one should not for comparison have recourse to information from the more well-to-do population in the country districts, from the peasant culture. Only the housing conditions of the unpropertied class in the country districts, which were not much better, and as a rule worse, are comparable. What is important in this connection is also that the type of dwelling has on the whole been the same in both quarters (kitchen-cum-living-room or kitchen with one room). It formed the natural frame for the furnishing of the dwelling. The traditional style was therefore easily transferred from the country district to the industrial and urban communities and survived there. Workers' barracks in industrial settlements and tenements in the towns naturally also call for attention as social phenomena: the type of building was the cause of the development of a block of flats with its relations to the surroundings.

What has been said above applies also to questions pertaining to clothing and cuisine. In both cases one should not exaggerate the importance of the form criteria, although traditional phenomena should be followed. New, formerly completely unknown clothes are not, however, always merely a sign of lack of tradition. People may switch to the new attire also on account of its suitability for a purpose, so that it may soon become traditional within an occupational group. This applies above all to working clothes or costumes; in connection with casual or leisure attire some other factor may be just as tradition-forming, e.g. the norms of the group and so forth. In this case, too, one should not seek comparative material among the more well-to-do peasants in the country districts, comparisons should be made with the dressing habits of the poorer classes and young people in the countryside during the transitorial period. On the whole, however, such material is not available, and it should therefore once more be emphasized that at the same time as worker communities and towns are studied one should give attention to the conditions in the country districts during the same period, especially among the unpropertied part of the population.

Finally, I will just touch upon the question of customs and usages, of spare-time occupations and hobbies. If one wishes to describe the life-style and norms of the new groups the above-mentioned questions should, of course, be investigated. Here, too, the type and form criteria applicable in the peasant community should be left in the background and the main stress be laid upon the function of the phenomena in a new environment. The festival occasions of life may be thrown into relief by recollections and interview material. If the object of study is a small community (industrial settlement or urban quarter), recollections may be effectively checked by analysing other material. The dry data of parish registers concerning births, marriages and deaths may, for example, be utilized statistically by transferring these to punched cards for analysis.[17] The

---

[17] An investigation by J. Eenilä on "Change in the baptismal custom in Reso parish", where this method has been used, has been printed in "Turun Ylioppilas" XIII, Forssa 1967, pp. 9–51.

yearly festivals may be studied with the help of recollections and the many-sided material of the newspaper of archive material of various kinds, etc. In this connection, in the worker and urban milieu, a new factor enters which should not be overlooked: associations and clubs of various kinds and their activities. Associations have in this context been studied also outside Nordic ethnology.[18] The ethnologist ought, as Sven B. Ek has expressed it, to "pay attention to the role of the associations for the formation of folknorms and folk-values, but also for various external customs".[19] In several cases, moreover, the associations have taken over the roles of the old traditional youth-groups (cf. youth-clubs and sports clubs, workers associations, etc.), influenced the uses to which spare-time is put through organized excursions, feasts, etc. Especially the political workers' associations have also had a role as training centres for different kinds of activity for their most interested members.

The social culture has still other aspects (family life, upbringing, relations to neighbours and relatives, etc.) which must be passed over. The best material for throwing light upon these questions can be obtained by collecting memories.

CONCLUSION

In this article the author has writtten with reference to Finnish conditions and certain experiences from Finnish material, collecting work and investigations in Finland in the years 1959–67. Certain questions which were of great importance in ethnological research on the peasant culture were of lesser importance in the worker and urban culture. I referred above, for example, to the question of traditional types and forms and working methods. In the new context these do not afford similar possibilities of drawing definite culture-historical conclusions as to their distribution, variation, etc., to throw light on the milieu studied, i.e. the development of the peasant culture. Forms, types and methods have, of course, their importance also in the worker and urban milieu, chiefly because they afford possibilities of comparison with unpropertied classes in the country districts, with the peasant culture

[18] Cf. H. Bausinger, Vereine als Gegenstand volkskundlicher Forschung, *Zeitschrift für Volkskunde* **55**, 1959, pp, 98–104; R. A. Hrandek, Beiträge zur Kenntnis der Wiener Vereinslebens, *ibid.* 1958, pp. 205–19; H. Schmitt, *Das Vereinsleben der Stadt Weinheim an der Bergstrasse*, Weinheim, 1963. Cf. also R. Braun, *Sozialer und kultureller Wandel in einem ländlichen Industriegebiet im 19. und 20. Jahrhundert*, Erlenbach–Zürich, 1965, pp. 297 ff.

[19] Sven B. Ek, Inför ett nytt startförsök (On the threshold of a new departure), *Folkliv*, 1964–5, p. 148.

and also with the culture of the higher classes. Also on the basis of these comparisons culture-historical conclusions may be drawn to throw light upon the development of the worker and urban culture. In order to attain this goal it is often, however, necessary to collect relevant material for comparisons; and it is therefore important that the collecting work should not be restricted solely to the worker and urban milieu, but be carried on also in the countryside in order to be able to throw light upon the conditions and trends of development there during the period of transition (about 1880–1914 from the Finnish point of view). Both the peasant class and the artisans, but especially the unpropertied class, must here be taken into consideration.

In the worker and urban culture there are certain phenomena (and their number increases with the passage of time) which from the viewpoint of form and type are not traditional in the ordinary sense. These cannot, either, be used for analysis of the kind indicated above, as comparative material from other social groups is not available. From the functional point of view, on the other hand, their importance in the culture-context to which they belong is not less than that of the older phenomena. This contrast between the traditional and the new, which has influenced not only the views of the layman, but also of the researchers, may be bridged over if in studies of worker and urban culture one consistently takes as one's point of departure the ecological and social structure and the function of the different phenomena in their culture. This does not mean that the concept of tradition is to be abandoned in the new investigations. Nor are form-typology and methods an independent goal in studies of the peasant culture; they are only a means for the characterization of the actual conditions of life and its historical development, the different norms and social connections in the milieu of the country district. The same ought to be the goal of ethnology also when one deals with studies of the worker and urban culture.

The peasant culture, the urban culture, the worker culture and so on, are only the different branches of the folk-culture that forms the all-round equipment for man's existence, although in the different milieus and on different ecological grounds it has acquired its special stamp. Studies of man's work and living milieu should therefore be the first and most important tasks.[20] If one has elucidated these, one can, with the help of different kinds of material, penetrate deeper and aim the writing of real monographs on groups communities and occupations.

[20] Cf. the works mentioned in note 6.

ETHNOLOGICAL RESEARCH AND TEACHING AT THE UNIVERSITY OF JYVÄSKYLÄ

Asko Vilkuna

Institute of Ethnology, University of Jyväskylä

1. THE NUCLEUS OF THE RESEARCH AREA

The center of the administrative district of Central Finland, Jyväskylä is located in the center of the population of Finland, somewhat north of the place where three large water routes empty into the northern end of Finland's longest lake, Päijänne.

From the middle ages up to the end of the 15th century western Finnish Tavastians traveled along these routes to their hinterland territories to hunt, fish and tax the Lapps, then still living in Central Finland. This manner of hinterland exploitation was given up only after a permanent settling of the territories began from the East. The eastern Finnish Savolax had learned a new slash and burn technique in the middle ages, with the help of which the coniferous forests could be made to produce grain. At the beginning of the new era they quickly took over for themselves the principal part of Central Finland, replacing the Lapps and the Tavastians. The eastern culture area expanded and froze to its present extent in the 17th century. The ethnological boundary between East and West Finland, which still can be observed today, was established at this time. At this boundary in Central Finland the fixed Tavastian agricultural settlement and the former Savolax culture based on the slash and burn clearing of coniferous forests meet each other.

Up to the 1860's Central Finland was hinterland. The most important commercial and cultural centers were located far away on the coasts. But then the situation changed. The monopoly of the coastal cities weakened due to the railroads, canals, St. Petersburg trade and industrialization, and politics which favored the inland parts of the country. Higher *Finnish-speaking culture* was now even officially acknowledged which, among other things, led to the situation in which one of the main strongholds of the new culture received its location in Jyväskylä, which from time to time competed successfully with the capital city for the position of the Finnish-speaking cultural center.

Economically Central Finland was enriched by the strong rise in the price of lumber in the 1870's. The forests on the area have always belonged to the best of Finland and they are located on good water routes for floating the logs. Much lumber was sold and at the same time wood-processing plants were founded in the vicinity of Jyväskylä. The city of Jyväskylä, founded in 1837, had until this time languished, which can be seen from the fact that its population by 1860 was only 900. Soon there-after a period of strong economic growth and cultural expansion began which has, with a few exceptions, lasted to the present time and raised the population figures to 55,000 (1967).

The boom period caused by the lumber led to changes in the structure of the economic pursuits in the countryside, to the rise of the level of agriculture, to the acceptance of innovations, and to the sharpening of class differences. Those households with a small area of cultivated land, dependent mostly on slash and burn agriculture, had few or no tenant farmers. The workers of a slash and burn company were independent wage earners, who lived in the households as dependent lodgers. When the forests were divided among the households, i.e. to those who had at least some land, and when, due to the rise in the price of lumber, slashing and burning was no longer profitable, the position of the dependent class weakened, especially since a change from natural to money economy took place at the same time. The incipient industry, and the lumbering with the log-floating work bound the landless population, but often only for a part of the year and with small wages. Great numbers of the dependent lodgers were left to live almost idle in the households, but also without income. On the other hand, the owners of the forests grew richer and richer and some were, on account of their wealth, quite comparable with the upper classes of the parish. Many were unable to handle their sudden-earned riches, but fell into an adventurous way of life, of which folklore and other documents give a parallel, but slightly different, picture.

The prosperity of Central Finland during the period of independence has been furthered by the strategic industries located there. After the Second World War emigrés from the shores of Ladoga moved into the province, among whom are Greek Orthodox believers who have their own churches and congregations in Central Finland. The life of the province has been especially strongly invigorated by the formation of the area into its own administrative district in the year 1960. The new administrative district is the most compact administrative unit in Finland, whereas Central Finland earlier was very fragmented administratively; the main part of the area belonged to the coastal administrative district of Wasa, bounding the Gulf of Bothnia, and ecclesiastically, until 1923, to the bishopric of the city of Borgå on the Gulf of Finland. Still in the 1950's Central Finland was called, though without reason, Northern Tavastland, a fact which can also be observed from school maps showing the provinces.

The provincial league of Central Finland is one of the liveliest in Finland. A couple of years ago they initiated a most noteworthy attempt in Finland in the field of tourism, including vacation villages and other activities.

2. ETHNOLOGY IN THE TEACHERS' COLLEGE AND THE UNIVERSITY OF JYVÄSKYLÄ

In 1858 Finland's first Finnish-language secondary school was founded in Jyväskylä, in 1863 Finland's first college for elementary school teachers and a year later Finland's first Finnish-language college preparatory girls' school. Of these, especially the teachers' college took it upon itself to preserve folk culture and educate people about it. The instructors owned newspapers and periodicals as well as presses and publishing houses. In the year 1863 the Society for the Advancement of Public Education, which has a significant place in the cultural history of Finland, was founded in Jyväskylä.

The level of the teachers in the teachers' college was high. From the point of view of ethnology the most important of the teachers was the architect Yrjö Blomstedt, who started the teaching of drawing and handicrafts at the institute in 1898. He was a widely-traveled courageous reformer and an inspiring teacher, a genuine national romantic who, according to his motto, "Back to nature and back to the antiquity of the Finnish people," admired *Kalevala*-ism and Karelianism, which, at that time, were seen to represent the most genuine and noble aspects of Finnish culture. Blomstedt was interested in folk building styles and forms of ornamentation and in folk culture in general. During his first year of activity he accomplished the fact that regional research, especially museum work, was taken over as official work of the convention of the college. With his students he made ethnological field trips into the surroundings to draw old objects, to collect folklore and to gather objects for the ethnological museum established in conjunction with the college in 1900. Permanent space was given to the museum in a Jugend-style, Karelian-inspired sculpture and drawing classroom building drawn up by Blomstedt and finished in 1905. Blomstedt's student, Samuli Paulaharju, received an ethnological awakening under his influence and has remained beside Lönnrot as the most noted collector of folklore. It should also be mentioned that Blomstedt in the year 1907 took the first steps to get the central Finnish Niemelä cottage to be moved to Seurasaari as the "foundation" for the establishment of a national outdoor museum.

At the efforts of Albert Hämäläinen and A. M. Tallgren, the museum of the College was in 1932 put in shape in conformity with the requirements of the times. Hämäläinen, a professor of Finno-Ugric ethnology at the University of Helsinki, was from Central Finland and studied his own home province, about whose buildings he has written a study, as well as one about the houses of the forest-Finns who moved to the central parts of Scandinavia from Central Finland. Instructor Toivo Ojala continued to increase the holdings of the museum to the extent that the founding of the Museum of Central Finland was made possible. A museum designed by Alvar Aalto was dedicated in 1961. Sirkka Valjakka (M.A.), the daughter of Ojala, acts as director of the museum.

To preserve its leading position in Finland the College has developed continually. In 1912 a scientific library, which has the right to free copies from the publishers, was established. In the same year the first summer university in Finland began, organized by the Finnish Academy of Sciences, and with Kaarle Krohn as one of its founders. At first it was meant to be primarily a teachers' college. In addition to subjects related to pedagogy, its main educational objects have included the folk-sciences. Several Estonian and Hungarian scientists have been included among its teachers. When the college was changed, in 1934, into a school of pedagogy which required a university examination for admission, the summer university was included as a third semester. Although Finland at present has seventeen summer universities, the one in Jyväskylä is the best recognized among them.

In the year 1958 a faculty was established at the College, but already by 1944 the program had included candidate's and doctor's examinations in pedagogy. In 1966 the name of the College was changed to a University and in the following year the Parliament passed a law on the University of Jyväskylä, which would contain, from 1968 on, four colleges and a teachers' school. In 1967 there were 3800 students, of which 7% were in the teachers' school. In Finland, those students who are working on the requirements in Finnish language have to take one course in ethnology and one course in folklore; earlier they had to pass the lowest requirement (approbatur) in one or the other. The history students at the University of Jyväskylä likewise have a one-semester course in ethnology. Since the subject is also elective in the teachers' school and in addition great num-bers of the teachers of design; home industry and handicrafts, whose instructor requirements include an approbatur in ethnology, study there in the summer, the teachers of ethnology and folklore from the University of Helsinki began to lecture, though not regularly, on their subjects at the University of Jyväskylä and to accept approbatur work.

From the fall semester of 1964 the University has had a professor's chair in the study of Finnish and Comparative Folk-Life. Under this heading come two different subjects for which certification is also given separately, namely in Finnish and Comparative Ethnology and in Finnish and Comparative Folklore (the latter up to a cum laude approbatur). The plan is to unite the subjects later and already seminar sessions are held in common.

Along with the Chair goes the Institute of Ethnology which will move, together with the Institute of Art History, into the previously mentioned building drawn up by Blomstedt, which has been thoroughly restored and repaired.

In addition to the professor, two assistants, an instructor and a temporary researcher are active at the Institute. Since more courses are taken during the summer at Jyväskylä in ethnology than anywhere else in Finland and since the Institute of Ethnology is concentrating chiefly on field work which is primarily done in the summer, the increase in the efficiency of the summer work has been taken into consideration in the program. In this respect the positions of one assistant professor and one secretary have been suggested, in which case the staff of the Institute would direct and teach during two semesters of the year and could take the third semester for research.

3. THE FACTORS WHICH HAVE AFFECTED THE RESEARCH PROGRAM OF THE ETHNOLOGICAL INSTITUTE OF THE UNIVERSITY OF JYVÄSKYLÄ

When the Institute of Ethnology began functioning, archives of folklore and ethnology were lacking at Jyväskylä. The object collection of the local museum was limited and the main library was not arranged with the needs of an ethnologist in mind. Since the central archives of national sciences located in Helsinki are difficult to copy and since these collections do not match the original sources, educational centers, such as Jyväskylä, have to utilize the results of field work in doing student studies. In this respect Jyväskylä is ideal as an area center for ethnological research. As a local university, it is still in connection with its surrounding country-side and among its students the positive influence of the local milieu can be seen.

In assigning field tasks for student work there is the additional advantage that the material so collected is immediately analyzed and archived under the supervision of the staff. More commonly, collected material is left in the archives, merely catalogued, but not set in its natural connections, a fact which is difficult to correct later. In joining the field work and re-search of the student the additional advantage is also achieved that for future field work trained manpower will be available. The so-called "outdoor orientation" is so prevalent among the student studies that about 9/10 of them are done on the basis of the students' own field collections.

As a matter of considerable significance, the Institute of Ethnology has participated in a cross-disciplinary study by a group of scientists investi-gating the effect of the border in the Tornio river valley. The last year of research will be 1969. All the humanistic sciences which do field work: ethnology, folklore, linguistics, sociology, cultural and economic geo-graphy and even community planning have taken part. The discussions of the different branches of science have proven fruitful and profitable to the methodology of one's own field. It is already noticeable that certain disciplines have adopted research methods from others. The Jyväskylä Institute of Ethnology strives after more cross-disciplinary research.

In drawing up the research program the Institute of Ethnology has checked the share of its own research in Finland so that all other research institutes working in the same field have been taken into consider-ation.

Finland has at the present time chairs related to folk-life studies in ethnology and folklore in three different cities. A certain division of labor among these fields is of course the natural starting point for research. As the Swedish-Finnish institutes have their own clearly demarcated area, which does not touch Jyväskylä, the programs of these institutes in Helsinki and Turku are not included. On the basis of the division of Finnish research subjects we can see that Helsinki with its National Museum and Seurasaari Outdoor Museum, with their network of collec-tors, and other central archives primarily represent research covering the entire country. The task of the Ethnological Institute of Helsinki and of the Seurasaari Foundation belonging to it, and the Ethnological Depart-ment of the National Museum, as well as that of the Folklore Archives of the Finnish Literary Society has to be seen, among other things, as the organizing of inquiries concerning the entire country. Ethnological research in Helsinki is directed strongly by the rich museum material, which directs interest to the traditional peasant culture, material objects and the past. Subjects such as the Finnish village, the peasant home, the stylistic features of folk furniture and the dating of popular ornament styles and relating them to their foreign connections have been characteristic of this research. Research on buildings has in its different aspects been in an important position for years. In addition to its nation-wide concerns the ethnology of Helsinki appears to have centered especially on Southern and Western Finland, i.e. to Finland's traditionally agrarian area.

Turku has stayed primarily in the milieu of Southwest Finland. Among its central research topics have been the sea with its different phenomena, the old city culture and the changes that can be detected in it, handicrafters' and loggers' traditions, as well as games.

Jyväskylä, accordingly, naturally gets for its share the Lake District and the eastern slash and burn culture area, their ethnic history and the movements of the population which have taken place in their sphere.

Common to all of course are the cultural changes with their innovations, urbanization, diffusion and on the other hand the study of different aspects of the old Finnish culture.

4. THE RESEARCH PROJECTS OF THE ETHNOLOGICAL INSTITUTE OF THE UNIVERSITY OF JYVÄSKYLÄ

On the basis of the field research already conducted and taking into consideration the already mentioned cultural geographical location of Jyväskylä, the Ethnological Institute of the University of Jyväskylä has temporarily fixed for its research program a somewhat modern direction which differs from the earlier Finnish, almost antiquarian directed, ethnological research. In the first place the object of study is the entire question of how the people in the country, in the settlements, and in the cities have adapted to, and live in the local milieu in creating from it a unique whole. Further the adaptation of the old agriculturally centered folk culture to the industrialized society is studied and the most characteristic factors which have affected the present culture entity are sought and an attempt is made to analyze their significance from the point of view of society, community, group and individual. In adapting to the milieu the mutual influence of the landscape, man and society has been taken as one of the central factors in the foreground.

The nearest research field is the Province of Central Finland. Its unique old folk culture is rich. At present the province is marked by rapid industrialization and the growth of settlements, but at the same time it has a few features characteristic of the so-called developing areas. As it is, the province offers a representative sample from the whole of Finland.

The research program now presented is of course hypothetical and it will never be realized as such. On the other hand it is a norm and it is hoped that by utilizing it, at least some kind of overview could be reached and the internal relations of different causal factors could be understood, i.e. for the most part generally accepted results could be achieved.

The Research Program

A. The research areas naturally belonging to the Institute due to the location of Jyväskylä (the research of the Lake District and of the Slash and Burn District)

1. The changes in the movements of the folk

   a. From a water-traffic parish to a highway parish
   b. The replacement of muscle power by motorized power in travel and traffic
   c. The determination of the economic areas (culture areas) according to the travel connections
   d. The horse as an important factor in the formation of folk life
   e. The birth of summer villas and their spread as reflectors of stages of water traffic at various times

2. The changing of the rural landscape

   a. The ethnological definition of the landscape types
   b. The use of forests and the wooded site during the hunting period, the slash and burn period, field economy period, the first boom period of the lumber industry, after these
   c. The choice of dwelling sites in the slash and burn culture area and in the lake district, the situation of the house, the scenery from it, comparison with Northern and Central Scandinavia

3. A holistic study of a sample parish

   a. The accurate mapping of certain ethnological features in a narrow area, mostly from the sample parish (an in-depth study)

b. The continuation of folk tradition, especially of material culture (the research could serve the development of the tourist industry and the raising of its standards)
c. The themes of parts 1 and 2 could be adapted to the sample parish study

B. Other fields of study (can be adapted to Central Finland or elsewhere)

4. The border area (ethnological border, culture border) research
    a. Finland-Sweden border area study in the Tornio-river valley, the results of which will be further developed in the interior of Finland and of Sweden
    b. The study of the border between the slash and burn culture area and Bothnia
    c. The analysis of the East-West culture boundary in Central Finland
    d. The eastern and western influences in the Central Finnish folk culture.

5. The study of the assimilation process
    a. The assimilation and adaptation of the rural folk in the city
    b. The assimilation and adaptation of the Greek Orthodox and Ingrians in Central Finland

6. Housing and residence research
    a. The dwellings of industrial workers and their living habits
    b. Other housing and residence studies

7. Use of distant resources
    a. The mapping of the use of natural meadows
    b. The swamp in folk economy
    c. Studies of other uses of distant resources.

8. The modernization and motorization of primitive means of livelihood
    a. The modernization and motorization of fishing
    b. The modernization and motorization of reindeer keeping.

9. Studies of economic conditions
    a. The influence of economic conditions on the folk-life and culture in Central Finland
    b. The influence of the first boom period in lumber trade on folk life and culture and on the traditional social classes in Central Finland.

C. Research programs based on the above topics suitable for studies outside Finland

5. THE RESEARCH PROGRAMS OF THE ETHNOLOGICAL INSTITUTE OF THE UNIVERSITY OF JYVÄSKYLÄ AND STUDIES ALREADY COMPLETED

(a) The total effect of a certain basic natural component in the formation of culture (lake as the first objective)

The kind of research presented here has not to our knowledge been carried out anywhere else in Finland. In examining the cultural phenomena caused by the Finnish lake, the fishing equipment, their manufacture and technical features have been thoroughly described, but in examining their use no attention has been paid to the biology of the fish, the eco-system of the lakes, or to the position of fishing in the totality of the annual folk-economy, or to the basis of the different fishing procedures. In the same fashion studies have been made, e.g. of the church-boat trips, but other traffic on the lakes and church trips in the winter have been left unnoticed. In examining the influence of a certain natural component on the culture as whole in the manner described below a tenable back-ground is created for ethnological and other cultural phenomena.

In Finland, the land of thousands of lakes, the lake and lake scenery are practically in the position of national symbols. Research aiming at the thorough explanation of the folk use of the lakes and their valuation can be assumed to possess a broad national significance which is not limit-ed to a narrow coterie of scientists, but maps the way for the scientific measurement of the native land's basic values. At the same time this kind of research is natural and pertinent Finnish ethnology. And as, in addition, the research is performed interdisciplinarily, it serves the different branches of science and in the best instances it leads to certain generally accepted results.

In planning the research subject in 1968, contact has already been es-tablished with district planning, natural conservation officials, tourist re-presentatives, a certain widely circulated illustrated journal, a publish-ing house radio and television (from the point of view of making a docu-mentary program and preserving films) and preliminarily with the hydro-biological institute founded in Jyväskylä in 1968.

In choosing the site of research we have worked together with the local planning league and the provincial league. The chief site for the research is Summasjärvi (järvi=lake) of the Saarijärvi parish where the basic hydro-logical features have already been thoroughly explained. Studies concern-ing limnology and ownership of the shores have also been performed.

Being of reasonable size, the lake can be handled even by a small group of researchers. On the other hand, it is large enough to have the different modes of folk usage of the lake occur adequately and representatively. The ecosystem of the lake and the natural and economic position of its shores well represent a typical lake suitable as a mean for the Lake District. In its sphere of influence concentrated shore village habitation as well as hill and scattered habitation can be found.

So that the lake research would reach a maximum scientific and national representativeness a decision has been made to adapt certain themes used in the Summasjärvi lake research to the study of a couple of small lakes found in the vicinity. For objects, on the one hand, a small lake with luxurious vegetation, eutrophically tinged and surrounded by cultivation (Lautajärvi) and on the other hand, a barren humus-predominating dystrophic woodland pond, which is situated far from the settled area (Mallatlampi), have been taken. They have been used at least to some extent by economic concerns which belong to Summasjärvi's sphere of influence. So that the different aspects of the long-distance lake traffic and modes of fishing would be seamlessly joined in the study, on their part research will also be conducted at the large Pyhäjärvi, near Summasjärvi, which already has some of the characteristics of a large body of water, and which represents a more barren lake type than Summasjärvi and the lake scenery of a sparsely populated woodland. Thus it is possible to conduct as representative as possible a lake study on a reasonably small area which at the same time belongs to the same local culture and has a unified territory.

In comparison with the Lake District in general, there are plentiful literary sources and research materials on Saarijärvi parish. The municipality of Saarijärvi is also interested in the research.

The significance of the presented lake study from the point of view of developing theories and methods of ethnology is surely considerable. But the results of the lake study serve, in addition to science itself, also the rational development of tourism and its direction to a genuine world of values. In this connection the vacation village which is already rising and which will be serving the tourist industry of Summasjärvi should be mentioned. The research serves also the protection of fish and significant work aimed at the development of fishing which attempts have been made to strengthen, especially in Central Finland. The research also has points of contact with a problem which has aroused widespread interest, namely to whom belong the problems of the contamination of our lakes and its prevention, as well as the preservation and care of our lake scenery.

I. *Description of the lake:* size, surface-area, morphology, relative depths, currents, winds, waves, nature of the bottom; lake as part of the water system; the surroundings of the lake; the populace in the lake's sphere of influence; the lake ownership.

II. *Ecosystem of the lake:* the quality of the water (the system's water type, water brought by tributaries and streams, sewer water from habitation); the changes in the surface of the water (annual, previous, lowering of the lake); vegetation; plankton; kinds of fish, other aquatic animals, water birds, their biology, species.

III. *Traffic:* Boat and ship routes; ports and havens, loading and unloading sites; seine sheds; docks; fixed points of traffic; connection with highways; the observation of travel on summer, marked and unmarked winter roads; the travel of inland dwellers to the mainland; boats (rowboats, motorboats, and their types), quantity, frequency of use, purpose of use, changes in usage and manufacture; flat-bottomed boats, canoes, ferries; winter traffic vehicles, quantity, frequency of use, purpose of use.

IV. *Fishing:* Sweep sites, reefs, depressions, spawning beds, reed beds; fishing gear; methods; fishing as a social factor (fishing companies and fishing communes); changes, their cause (price formation, new gear, relation of fishing to other means of livelihood, contamination); the annual cycle of fishing now and earlier; the evidence of inventories and other documents; information based on memory; wilderness fishing; preservation and use of fish, marketing; the regulation of fishing (limitations, stocking, education, legal regulations and their maintenance).

V. *Catching of other aquatic animals and water birds* (as above).

VI. *The use of other lake products:* lake ore; dyeing clay; stones for sauna and fireplaces; drift wood and sunken logs.

VII. *Dairying:* Pasturage (shores, rushes, islands); shore and alluvial meadows; dried areas, ditched areas; shore thickets (willow thickets); the use of reeds and rushes.

VIII. *The use of the water:* Washing and giving drink to cattle; the use of lake water in the household; sauna; laundry; soaking flax; sawing ice; freezing of lumber roads and storage sites.

IX. *Floating logs:* amounts; times; equipment; loggers; groups and companies.

X. *The lake as the determinator of the locale of buildings and household work sites:* the relations of the main and outhouses to the lake; the shore sauna, storehouse, hay barn; the laundering site.

XI. *The lake as a boundary and an obstacle on the one hand and as a uniting factor on the other.* The relationship of the administrative areas to the lake; allotments and changes in allotments; common waters; the lake as a traffic route and obstacle (from a waterway parish to a highway parish); the handicaps caused by the lake for the location of a center and for conducting business at the center.

XII. *The lake as a social factor and as a place to spend leisure time.* Summer places; shore cabins; tourism; dance platforms and kiosks; celebration of Midsummer; island treks; shore fishing and swimming.

XIII. *The mapping of the values related to the lake.* Significance to economic life and contentment (valuation and attitude); the share of the lake in the feeling for the home district; lake and artists.

XIV. *Traditions attached to the lake* (legends, beliefs, fishing and other magic).

XV. *Place names.*

XVI. *The position of the lake in local history.*

The lake study will not begin in earnest until 1969 when the University's external financing will be organized. So that the plan will be realized quickly, the furthering of the lake project was taken into consideration for some of the tasks assigned earlier. Thus one student, doing a laudatur-study of the saunas of two shore villages, has handled his object so that many of the questions related to the lake are illuminated. In addition, two laudatur-studies which treat the location of the house relative to the landscape are in preparation (one is from the lake shore villages, the other from the river-bank habitations). The purpose is to illuminate by factor-analysis those elements which have led to the situation of the dwelling and the yard in a certain place (factors include, among others, land owner-ship, cultivations, travel routes, relative altitude, soil, view, observation or following of outside life, shore, well, original dwelling, previous house site, such as a fishing cabin, services, neighborliness, sociability, compass directions, winds, drifting snow), in which case the relative scale of values between the factors and the changes that have taken place in it will be treated. For the purpose the buildings have been photographed as part of the landscape, as buildings and dwellings and as yard complexes; a card containing over a hundred details has been filled out.

To carry out the plan, trial studies have been assigned. For experimental purposes the staff of the Institute has prepared a study of the influence of a basic natural component, in this case a *swamp*, so that the methods to be used can be made pertinent from the point of view of the entire program.

In addition to the study of some other basic natural component it is possible to advance in other directions as well from the lake study. Thus for example the part treating lake traffic can be expanded to a study covering all folk traffic and its changes. Such themes for research as "the determination of cultural areas according to travel connections," "the replacement of muscle power by motor power in traffic," and "from a waterway parish to a highway parish" open up naturally from this foundation. The last mentioned is quite timely a theme in Finland since in the 1970's there will be a change to large municipal units. At the time of the birth of the parishes the lake was a connecting link between the villages, but in the period of cars and highways it has become an obstacle so that many of the parishes in the Lake District are now in a difficult situation with regard to getting services for their remoter inhabitants.

(b) The assimilation of a certain portion of the populace

In order to clarify the central problem of the entire program, "how the population of the rural areas, settlements and cities has adapted and adapts to the local milieu in creating out of it a unique entity and how the old agrarian-centered folk culture adapts to the industrialized society" the Institute of Ethnology has made a few limited studies concerning the adaptation of the 1944 immigrants into their new environment. In addition to this there is a broad study program under preparation about the dwellings of people who have moved from the country to the city, their living habits and their abandonment of the natural economy.

One of the studies concerns the survival of Karelian food preparation among the Orthodox living in Jyväskylä. In the Orthodox rural milieu in Karelia, foods were prepared in a manner differing greatly from the rest of Finland, and often demanding great work; many were related to certain events or feasts. Those interviewed for the study were divided into groups according to whether both man and wife in the household were Orthodox or whether one or the other was Lutheran. In addition widows and spinsters were interviewed. An attempt was made to find out how the age of the persons in question in the groups affected the preservation of the customs of preparing food. Observations were also made of the effect of becoming immigrants, of general changes in the preparation of foods, the changes in the food preparation surroundings, of the influence of the housewife's taking a job, of the present Orthodox feasts, ceremonies and bazaars, plus ethnocentric features attached to these plus the belief that "the way to a man's heart is through his stomach."

There is also another study of the Orthodox which examines how their great church holidays *(prasniekka)*, to which are attached a great deal of non-Christian mythological material, were secularized in the 1900's and finally disappeared in 1939, when the area was taken over by the Soviet Union.

In the studies of the merging of the Karelian Lutheran immigrants to the western Finnish agricultural milieu and its populace it has been noted that the relations between the two groups have normalized in about ten years and the uniquely Karelian features can be expected to be lost in about 30 years from the time of emigration.

The Institute of Ethnology began to study the living habits of the Jyväskylä workers in 1967. For the first object the dwellings and living habits of certain paper mill workers, and the changes which have taken place in them in this century were chosen. Of the 600 workers of the mill founded in 1872 half live in housing owned by the mill, whereas the other half live either in their own, or housing rented from other individuals.

In this sense an attempt is made to form a picture of the development of the central-Finnish factory worker's housing. The following factors will be described: the outside appearance and shape of the houses, their size, number of rooms, the furnishing of the kitchen and chamber and their use, outhouses, garden and natural economy. At the same time the differences between one's own place and the housing furnished by the factory will be compared as well as those between a bachelor and a family dwelling. The housing policy of the factory administration is also significant (the allocation of lots to the workers, the rental level of the factory housing, the right to live in factory housing, the social building policy practiced by the factory), the influence of the city on the housing conditions of the workers and the location of the housing in the city in regard to the factory and services. The purpose here is to collect information on the disappearing old housing culture in the city undergoing strong renewal and at the same time study assimilation processes. Special stress is laid on how the workers came to the city, the customs they brought with them, habits and material culture, their attitude toward the former home in fishing and other work assistance trips, visits to relatives, food purchases and, on the other hand, how the country relatives visited and received quarters in the city. In a central position is also the problem of how the working family in the city used cattle, garden, orchard, food preservation and how this old natural economy as well as the homemade furnishings of the house and homemade clothing has disappeared and is disappearing. The renaissance of the natural economy caused by World War II also is a part of this question.

All the dwellings have been measured, color-photographed inside and out, the inhabitants have been interviewed and the archives have been gone through. Four smaller studies and one laudatur-study have been completed. The material will be handled during 1968 so that a concentrated program can be put together for subsequent objectives, for making comparisons and deepening the understanding of the problems involved.

In this phase special attention will be paid to how the influence of this kind of milieu on an outside individual can be expressed. Much can be gleaned from photographs, archives and interviews, but on the basis of the same materials this could also be expressed later. But later the spirit of this way of living could not be recaptured, that feeling which the teacher's son, the student who has grown up in a rural home or the scholar who has traveled in different environments, gets while traveling in and becoming acquainted with the worker's milieu.

(c) The influence of factory-made objects on the formation of folk-culture

The Finnish ethnology dealing with material culture has almost solely paid attention to handmade objects, which have in addition to the individual maker an individual form, i.e. they are "folk" products. But when the coffee pot bought from the parsonage auction moves from the upper class to its peasant surroundings, then even a factory-made object in its folk surroundings is an organic part of the whole. Although there is probably no need always to study the forms of these objects deeply, they have to be otherwise noted, especially when they have thoroughly shaken the traditional ways of life. On the part of many factory-made objects it is possible, on the basis of only memory accounts to form a picture of its acceptance as a novelty, its assimilation to the culture and finally its replacement. For the students who were born in the 1940's, the interest in the study of these things may be greater than for some more traditional items, which they have never seen operating. At least with the help of these factory-made objects it will be easy to build a bridge to the earlier elements which fulfilled a comparable function.

In Finland cattle-keeping is traditionally woman's work. In the forest village under study this strict division of labor between the sexes was first shaken by the first and following *separators* brought there. It was at this time that the men considered machines to belong to the men's sphere and began to use the separator. The interest of the men could already then have caused the destruction of the old division of labor had not the women, proud of the first machine which eased their heavy work load, practically driven the men from the handle of the separator. In addition, the men's traditional tasks presumed long periods away from home, during which the milk also had to be handled. In the beginning the women used the separator with a pious attitude toward their work, indicated, for example, by singing hymns while separating the cream. Later the separator became a mere useful tool in the larger houses, but to the smaller it represented a certain status symbol which was bought at an auction at an excessive price for an uneconomical use. It was not until the advent of the next machine, the *milking machine*, that the old division of labor was given up. But when it was accepted the old society had already changed. The separator is no longer used, but the milk is taken in the morning with a rubber-tired cart to a roadside platform for the dairy truck to pick it up. If the village has a common platform, an informal "village parliament" meets there every morning, the nightly meetings of which the TV programs have made less possible, and many of the old meeting places have moved to the settlements or disappeared.

The *bicycle* appeared in the flatland agricultural parish studied, whose population sensitively follows conjunctures, at the end of the 19th century. The pharmacists, teachers and storekeepers of the parish bought bicycles, whereas carpenters and smiths made them experimentally of wood and iron. There were several of these "folk" bicycles. Because of its novelty and expense the bicycle was well-cared for and one might even dress up when going to see one. The rise in status of a bicycle owner partly caused its rapid spread, but it was not until the 1920's that its use spread to all circles and in the 1930's it was common even among the workers. By then the wealthiest in the village already owned a car or a motorcycle and the bicycle had become a commonplace. The 1930's and 1940's were the heydays of the bicycle; in the 1950's the motor scooter had replaced it and in the 1960's the car is becoming all-ruling, although recently the bicycle has revived due to bicycle races and due to its ergometric properties. Those with little means and living a long distance away beyond bad roads have been most faithful to the bicycle. The comparison of men's and women's bicycles illustrates the position of the woman in a changing society. At the beginning of the century the bicycles sold were almost entirely men's bicycles and used only by men. Reasons for this were the high cost of bicycles, the mobility of men and the woman's adherence to the home circle, the awkward long skirts of the women, rules of propriety, the conservativeness of women, and the men's interest in "machinery". In the 1930's an equivalent amount of men's and women's bicycles were sold, but during the last ten years, after the men's acquisition of different motor vehicles, the bicycles have been mostly women's models and used primarily by women and children. In the study the number of bicycles present at different times beside the church fence, in the schoolyard, and at dances has been counted. Those coming from the outlying villages have given up the use of the bicycle for attending dances; they leave their vehicles a few kilometers away and drive the rest of the distance with a taxi.

The study brought out how the bicycle has influenced the *increased mobility of the population* (the increased trips to the stores by the outlying villagers, the increase in turnover, the increase in the number of visits, although the purchases at a time may have decreased, the bicycle as a means of transport), dance, gathering and church trips have increased and extended to a broader area. The bicycle has, in addition, *increased the contacts* not only for the old, but also *for the young*, and it has had a decisive influence in extending the area for the choice of a marriage partner. The bicycle has also *increased the possibility of getting work*, for the significance of the distance to work has diminished. *The bicycle is a partial factor in social mobility*, for it has increased the number of children attending secondary school from the outlying villages; poor parents could not afford living quarters in the settlement for their child, but could give him a bicycle to use. Perhaps the bicycle has also been to a small extent responsible for the disappearance of the inns.

In 1966 all 16 houses were studied in one lake shore village. Of these, one was a large house, while the others followed the pattern: living room + vestibule + chamber. The purpose of the research was to ascertain the age of the chamber, its origins and functions. At the beginning of the century the room, separated from the living room by the vestibule, served as a storage room for food and other things, less often as a temporary bedroom. In the 1930's it became a heatable chamber which had the function of a parlor. It was rarely heated. Only after the coming of the *television* which was, without exception, placed in this room, did the chamber come into everyday use. The same phenomenon is observable in the dwellings of the Jyväskylä workers which consist of a kitchenette, chamber and a vestibule (normal type). Television has also encouraged changes in the furniture to facilitate watching.

In the 1960's in the northern parts of the country and especially in the northern most reindeer breeding areas of Lapland, a certain completely factory-made invention, the snowmobile, has appeared to be an element strongly affecting the people's means of livelihood. The Ethnological Institute of the University of Jyväskylä has aided the research of the University of Minnesota Anthropological Institute (Professor Pertti Pelto) which has centered on the influence of the snowmobile on reindeer herding and its indirect influence on the structure of the economic and social field in Finnish Lapland. Certain trends have already been detected in the research:

In reindeer herding there has always been room for old men, wise in the ways of reindeer and knowledgeable of the habits of both animals and men. Until the snowmobile revolution, the older generation had not been pushed aside by the trends of change. Now, however, with the snowmobile, it is mostly the younger generation that commands the skills. Because of the increased costs due to the snowmobiles the reindeer keepers are forced to butcher more reindeer than previously. For those owning a few reindeer this may mean the end of reindeer-keeping possibilities. The snowmobile may lead to a stronger specialization in reindeer keeping. The number of reindeer per owner will have to be larger than previously. Those with few reindeer will have to give up reindeer breeding as a means of livelihood, or serve as mere wage earners in place of a previously independent existence.

In the associations of the reindeer owners in the southern part of the reindeer-breeding area, where the numbers of the herds are small and where reindeer-breeding is a minor sideline, hardly any snowmobiles are in use in reindeer herding.

The study is also of interest from the point of view of general ethnological research concerning movements and traffic. Especially in the northern areas, the individual's need to move rapidly over a wide area is the greatest, due to the necessities of livelihood.

The increased mobility of individuals due to the use of the snowmobile appears to have fostered an increase in recreational and social activities, too.

(d) Other studies

In addition to the habitation studies presented above, attention has also been directed to *urbanization:* the development from horse drivers to taxis; from keeping of cattle in the city to the abandonment of the practice; the income and activities of a florist business, funeral home, and photographer; name-day and birthday customs; confirmation and wedding dresses.

The contacts between the rural and city folk during markets and in connection with marketplace life has also been studied. Among other things it has been noted that at least in some cities a regular institutionalized

12

quartering-relationship was formed between certain city and rural households, which led to the creation of other contacts also, even up to important economic ones, e.g. the city dweller's cows might be kept in summer
pasturage with the market-lodger from the country. Family relationships
aided quartering relationships, but this was by no means the only, nor
even the main factor in determining the formation of the relationship.
The income derived from rented lodging has had considerable significance
to the city dwellers.

   Some studies have been made of the *changes in the living surroundings.*
A ground plan has been drawn up of certain houses, the main dwelling
as well as outbuildings. All the rooms of the main building have been
inventoried along with their furniture, textiles, flowers, etc. Photography
has been used as an aid. With the help of knowledge based on memory,
documents, old photographs and other sources, the changes in the living
space and personal property which have taken place during 50–90 years
have been described. A history of the house has been made, with personal
information, property divisions, changes in professions and so forth,
for the same period. In this fashion an attempt has been made to place
the changes in the house plans and personal property in an historical
connection:

Year	*History*	*House*	*Personal Property*
1912	Daughter-in-law A.N. moved into the house	The old couple moved into the chamber, door G. was opened.	A.N. brought with her ..., ... was taken to the chamber

(in reality the description is much more detailed). At the same time attention has been paid to the relationship of bought, inherited and self-made
objects, to fashion trends, changes in social relations, etc. It is surprising
to note how many changes the house, which from the outside appears
very static, has experienced in a very short time, while its inhabitants have
attempted to adapt to the requirements of the new conditions.

   In one study an outlying village's *gift-giving institution* was observed
to have changed greatly in a few decades. Engagements are no longer
regarded as the beginning of marriage, so that wedding gifts have to some
extent replaced engagement gifts. The bride moves directly to her husband's home, so that the gifts of the earlier in-between phases have been

left out. The marriage has become a matter for the couple only and not for the entire family, so that the gifts which used to be given to the relatives have been eliminated. The name-gifts of the child earlier formed an important basic capital for the child, but the rise in the standard of living and in social security has decreased their significance. Nowadays, even the everyday food is sufficiently rich so that the valuation of delicacies as gifts has decreased. On the other hand, the quantity of goods has increased many times due to the increase in the standard of living (formerly food used to be brought to a house where a funeral was being held, now silk bedcovers, etc. are brought). Purchased presents have become more general due to the increase in stores and the choice of goods available, the decrease in manpower and skills plus the rural attitude that the factory-made is better than hand-made. The upper classes have brought new gift-giving occasions to the main village which later spread to the outlying villages; the quantity of Christmas gifts and their significance has grown, nameday and birthday gifts have become common only after World War II. The latter are supported by communication media and social leveling. Gathering of the gifts is done communally. Gift-giving still expresses a way of thinking characteristic to the villagers. The presents have to be utilitarian, e.g. flowers are not valued. The receiver always attempts to "pay his debts" when the opportunity arises. The gifts are considered trade goods. The basic thought is expressed by the saying: "One goes visiting by turns, seldom coming to one's own."

Social leveling has also caused the *disappearance of the pietist dress*. The old national costume was adopted in the agrarian milieu of a certain area as the pietist dress. Since World War II its use has continually decreased. The reasons for its disappearance are, above all, the loosening of religious absolutism, the spiritual and material crisis, caused by the war, in all its facets, (e.g. those who had served many years as comrades-in-arms no longer wished to be separated by dress after peace came), increased schooling which affected all layers of society (the pressure of other students), leaving the land, increased communal and other common activities. Likewise the expense of the suit is a factor, since inexpensive village tailors are no longer available. At the pietist meeting of 1942, most wore the dress, but during a comparable meeting in 1966, of the some 40,000 participants, only about 600–700 wore the dress.

The *living folk-tradition* of a village, which in 1966–67 proved to be a very important tourist center, was mapped and an attempt was made to find from it the material which might be useful for *tourism* so that the cultivation of the thoroughly quasi-folk-culture, which has occurred in so many tourist centers, would be avoided. Shoe gear, birch bark objects, woven materials, seine fishing, church-boat trips, shorefish food, native beer, old buildings and milieu, folk-music and logfloating have indicated promise.

In folklore and ethnology many studies have been made of *personalities*. The influential persons of a certain area have already been studied and their activities from the point of view of various social groups have been illuminated. Thus it has been noted in what different ways newspapers, archive material, literature, the minutes of the farming district meetings, colleagues, friends, neighbors, agronomists, servants and folklore tell of the great landowner. Or the folk healer has been studied and in this connection those living in the neighborhood and further off have been interviewed, the material of different archives has been studied as well as court records. In a few cases it has been interesting to note how folklore about them begins to be created, leading finally to fairly well-formed memorates and legends.

In the field of folklore several studies have been made from the world of school children, e.g. of the *opening rhymes of games*. Among the children the traditions are alive but separated from the adult world. Temporal comparisons are easy to carry out because the old people generally remember their childhood folklore and later times have not substantially changed its content. The school teachers have sympathetically acted as helpers.

In the field of folklore the study of the *hiisi—tradition* in the vicinity of a certain lake should also be mentioned. The *hiisi* is a mythological being, whose activities are often fixed to the terrain. In the lake's sphere of influence there are several places connected with the *hiisi*. In the study the favored features of the legends were studied in villages on different sides of the lake. At the same time comparisons were made as to what portion of the *hiisi* legends were known by different age groups, and where each had learned the *hiisi*-tradition. The local tradition of today was compared with that in the folklore archives of the Finnish Literary Society and information about the *hiisi* of the lake in the local newspapers and in a publication about the home area. The *hiisi* tradition, during the entire period of memoranda concerning it, has been maintained by factors other than a belief in the *hiisi*. The greatest portion of the memoranda have been made in a period when active telling had already been replaced by a passive knowledge about the *hiisi*. During the period of transition, the cause of the home area and various organizations have needed uniting programs tied to the community. This, as well as the *hiisi* legend told in schools in connection with teaching about the surroundings, has in part standardized the versions of different villages and families. As entertainment the *hiisi* legend has not withstood competition and it is not adequately fairytale-like to have sufficient significance as children's property.

(e) The teaching and research trends at the Ethnological Institute of the University of Jyväskylä ·

Jyväskylä is lacking central archives and museums, but a rich research area surrounds it. For this reason field work has achieved central importance. But because of the scarcity of archive materials and literature the handling of the field data has had to be limited to a short period of time, that limited by memory. Thus both research and education have concentrated on modern ethnology. From this perspective certain conclusions can already be drawn.

Ethnology, no doubt, has been at a crossroads in the 1960's. The ethnology of many capital cities has changed into an archive, literary or museum science, in which areas the majority of research assignments are handed out. It is probable that in this way ethnology will soon be in the same position as the study of folklore or archaeology which lack the opportunities for the study of phenomena in living surroundings.

A reason for this is in part the definitions given in certain articles, in the names of chairs, and so forth. Usually they are given by the old generation and reflect the directions of research and views of their authors. In receiving the seal of an article of belief they, though antiquarian, are strongly defended, which fact sometimes affects the development of ethnology negatively. The "harmonious agrarian society" (the peasant community) idealized by them is already past. But the research which still has the study of this society as its goal has restricted field research from striking out in new directions.

In the definitions given there is the general fault that they restrict a certain aspect of the science as ethnology, the boundaries of which are then zealously guarded by the intellectually rigid. Nevertheless, in modern times when the interdisciplinary direction is growing more useful, ethnology should move from the emphasis on its boundaries to the description of itself so that the other sciences would be able to recognize its position and know what kind of work they could do in common.

The strong points of ethnology are first of all, that it is able to combine horizontal and vertical lines of humanistic studies, the present time and tradition, field work and archive sources. Perhaps ethnology has been emphasized even recently as an only historical science. The advantage of ethnology is the ability to reach an all-encompassing vision. Differing from history or sociology, it is not satisfied with the sole use of "exact" sources, which may give a quasi-exact view of reality. Hardly any other science besides ethnology is able to create an all-encompassing picture of an ethnos, a description which catches the flavor of that difficult-to-capture spirit of time, place, and society which can be found in a similar fashion in some excellent old-time travel account. Thus ethnology can be characterized as the elucidator of the old and the new in a way which cannot be done with the present day archive materials, or as the author of unwritten literature. Observation, even when partly based on intuition, has a significant position, although it occasionally leads one astray.

Ethnology is also characterized by the fact that an ordinary person, whoever he may be, is of interest to it. Who would enjoy the company of an 18th-century man, from the viewpoint of science, as much as an ethnologist? But the same is true of the man of our century. His biography, regardless of his position, has source value to the ethnologist. Among field research the geographer most often passes by the man as an object of interview, the sociologist, on the other hand, does not interview him as an individual, but as a part of a mass, about carefully limited topics with limited possibilities for answers. The individuality of an individual is left to ethnology; the individual is of interest as an individual as well as a participant in his group and as a reflector of his group.

Some sciences working in the field treat their primary materials as being of transient worth; the primary material is not the most important thing in itself, but the direction for the development of society which may be deduced from it or the development of theories. On the contrary, an all-encompassing ethnological field work done with care is real basic research which will long maintain its source value.

In field research ethnology has been able to give a contribution to general science. This is why its field work methods have constantly to be developed. Although the majority of the field collections have been well made, it is possible to notice occasionally that, e.g. in the photograph collections of the National Museum the collectors have been too interested in the old harmonious agrarian community. Too wealthy is the culture of the upper classes, too poor the non-peasant. What has been photographed from the remaining homogeneous agrarian culture is the "representative", "old-fashioned", "genuine", "aesthetically emphasizing the peasant" or "special", which has perhaps been assumed to be a survival. This view has sometimes led to the situation that the 1930's village studies describe the 19th-century village and that in the 1950's, plans do not include the buildings younger than 30 years and that the questionnaires ask only of the past: "was it known?" or "was it the custom"?

In the ethnological field research of the 1960's in Finland an attempt has been made to preserve also the present time and to use exact collecting methods and to treat the objective as a whole. Since there are no possibilities for large basic researches, a sampling system has been developed, in which valuable help has been received from the geographers and sociologists. In new studies the national central archives have proven to contain gaps. In a situation like this, the sub-centers, such as Jyväskylä, can serve the central archives so that they will be able to fill the gaps with their questionnaires encompassing the entire country.

Although many of the studies of the Ethnological Institute of the University of Jyväskylä fall outside the scope of normal ethnology, e.g. the lake study, in which the starting point is an element of nature rather than that of culture, they still have the rationality that, by experimenting from all aspects, ethnology can outline a picture of the present.

For the students ethnology is one of the few humanistic disciplines which in part observe the society in its entirety. Modern students are more socially conscious than their elders, but traditional ethnology is surprisingly far from their realm of experience. The students should rather be led to the company of tradition through life, through city ethnology, field work, active outdoor museums and hikes. Field work has the advantage that its participants receive, at least in part, a concept of the manifold structure of society and learn to understand the significance of various aspects of culture, especially of tradition. When the material is handled by modern methods it follows that the people in question get acquainted with research methods. Since research continues to grow in importance and to all areas in our society, more and more general knowledge concerning research will be demanded of those who have received an academic education.

A strong ideology of help for the developing nations may be noticed among the students. Where the old generation of scholars studied primitive societies in order to find the factors which had influenced the birth and development of their own society, it would now be proper that the students in turn would get acquainted with the developmental processes of their own society, from a developing country to a civilized and industrialized society, so that they would, by the use of these models, develop the future of the developing nations. Signs can be seen that attempts are made to utilize general ethnology as one of the means of educating experts on developing nations.

Finally, we should note that certain present ethnological studies serve

the province and its nearby areas so that the attention of those participating officials and institutions will be directed to such important factors
as the channeling of tourism along proper lines, the conservation of landscape, and the rational and long-term planning of the use of natural resources, as well as the realization of the value of native culture. At the same
time materials and guidance can be given to planners of the community
and local areas.